19 71.

10/6

THE ENGLISH CARDINALS

THE ENGLISH CARDINALS

WITH SOME ACCOUNT OF THOSE OF OTHER ENGLISH-SPEAKING COUNTRIES

BY

G. C. HESELTINE

LONDON

BURNS OATES & WASHBOURNE LTD.

PUBLISHERS TO THE HOLY SEE

1931

NIHIL OBSTAT:

EDUARDUS J. MAHONEY, S.TH.D.,
Censor deputatus.

IMPRIMATUR:

EDM. CAN. SURMONT,
Vicarius generalis.

WESTMONASTERII,
die 1a Junii, 1931.

Made and Printed in Great Britain

TO

ALFRED GARDINER

FOREWORD

THERE is a thin red line of English Cardinals running through English history for the past eight hundred years. It is a line almost, but not quite, unbroken. It is a line that has linked England with the most continuous and influential power in Europe during that period. The link is not merely religious or ecclesiastical, it is also cultural and political.

The Cardinals, Princes of the Church, form the Cabinet or Executive Body. The permanent nature of the Church as a Power, temporal and spiritual, and a subtle indivisible combination of the two, has given the Cardinals a status in Europe, and now indeed over the whole world, comparable with that of the temporal rulers. The temporal powers of Europe have come and gone, dynasties have risen and fallen, now this and now that Power has been in the ascendant. But the College of Cardinals has an unrivalled continuity not only of personnel but of policy. In the weakest days of the Papacy it could not be ignored by the strongest Power.

Similarly whatever family or faction has ruled

England—Norman, Plantagenet, Tudor, Stuart or Hanoverian—whatever change has followed change—feudalism, despotism, monarchy, oligarchy—whether England has stood high in Europe as under Edward III and Henry VIII, or low as under John and James, there has always been, but for short unimportant intervals, an English representative not subject to such changes, in the executive of a more permanent Power, the Papal Curia.

These Englishmen, occupying so high and responsible a position in the European civilization (as well as in the Church which is the mystical Body of Christ), have all taken with them, as part of the English contribution to the culture and polity of Europe, the qualities of their English nature. For five centuries the religion of these men, the road whereon their high office was situate near the bridge-head, was as native to them, to all Englishmen and to England, as the English tongue and the English air. At the end of that time, when a foreign religion was imposed upon the English people and they were denied the Faith which had been their birthright ever since they had been civilized, this line of men, continuous only in their office, retained the whole Faith of their country and their fathers. The English Cardinals, more than any other line of men for so long a time, have remained Englishmen. Sometimes they have done so with such emphasis that they have been reviled for it, as for a crime. With very few exceptions they have been a credit to England. They have in turn equalled the best of their day in ability, virtue, wisdom and power. It is a strange fact, considering the frailty of all men and of Cardinals no less, that the Englishmen have excelled in the virtues but not in the vices of their kind. Very few of the half-hundred have been really bad, none bad enough to excel in vice or to rival the worst in their day.

For eight centuries the English Cardinals have had a direct effect on English history. In the first half of that period they exerted a direct and decisive influence on English affairs, both internally as statesmen and prelates and externally by their representation abroad. In the second half of the period their influence has been more restricted and indirect, but it has never been negligible. It would be a rash man or a bigot who could survey English history and oppose the view that the influence of the English Cardinals, compared with any other class of men, has been on the whole very much to the good, and that the decline in representation in the English College was a loss to England and the Church. The Church can stand it.

In this account the three Scottish Cardinals have been included with the Englishmen for the sake

of continuity, and with no intention of slighting
the great Scottish people. They can hardly consider the inclusion derogatory. The matter is no
doubt otherwise with the Irish, and possibly with
the Colonials and Americans, who may have good
reasons of their own for resenting such inclusion,
and their Cardinals are therefore given a separate
section.

Many dates and facts may be found to be at
variance with those given in the standard and more
popular books of reference, but not more so than
those works are at variance with one another. The
account here given has been compiled from contemporary sources as far as possible, and an effort
has been made to check more recent sources of
information.

G. C. H.

CONTENTS

xiii

CONTENTS

PART III

IRISH, AMERICAN AND COLONIAL CARDINALS

LIST OF ILLUSTRATIONS

PART I. 1143–1530

CATHOLIC ENGLAND

CHAPTER I

THE POPE'S MEN

I. ROBERT PULLEN

BEFORE the Norman Conquest, the isolation of England, its unstable social organization, its political insignificance in the European system and its comparative lack of educational facilities, may have been responsible for the lack of Englishmen in high places in the government of the Church. That Englishmen did distinguish themselves in the Church is shown, for example, by the position held by Alcuin of York in the Court of Charlemagne, when the empire and rule of that monarch was very closely identified with that of the Papacy. But from the time of the appearance of the Cardinalate as such until the reign of Stephen, we have no records of Englishmen in that office.

The first Englishman whom we know to have been created Cardinal was Robert Pullen, who was also called Robert le Poule. That may have meant, as some say, Robert the Chicken, for the twelfth century was not without its humour,

3

but it is more probable that the name was derived from his supposed birthplace, Poole, in Dorset. He is first heard of teaching philosophy and logic for some five years at Oxford, one of the earliest masters there, having many pupils, including John of Salisbury, who later distinguished themselves. Oxford owes much to Pullen for the prestige which he gave to the place when it was a university in embryo. From Oxford he went to Paris, where he taught with great success and became the friend of S. Bernard of Clairvaux, whom he supported vigorously against the heresies of Abelard. S. Bernard wrote about him in very flattering terms to the Bishop of Rochester, whose archdeacon he was.

In 1141 the now famous Robert Pullen went to Rome at the call of Pope Innocent II. Two years later Pope Celestine created him Cardinal, and in the next year he was made Chancellor of the Holy See by Pope Lucius II. Six centuries were to elapse before an Englishman again occupied that office. As Chancellor, Pullen was more than chief administrator of the papal possessions, for his jurisdiction covered the whole of the Christian world. In this capacity he showed good business acumen and considerably increased the papal revenues. He was generally acknowledged to be well-mannered, cultured and wise, of unblemished reputation. He died about 1147.

In his best-known work, *Sententiarum Logicarum*, against heretics, he relied on scripture, reason and papal decisions rather than on the appeal to tradition or precedent. No doubt his presence at Rome paved the way for the Englishmen who were to follow him, and it is more than likely that he influenced the Pope in favour of Nicholas Breakspear.

II. NICHOLAS BREAKSPEAR

It was in 1146, whilst Pullen was Chancellor of the Holy See, that the Canons Regular of S. Rufus, near Valence, complained for the second time against the severity of the rule of their Abbot. This disciplinarian, who had entered the convent as a lay-brother, was Nicholas Breakspear. Pope Eugenius III, who by this time knew something of his career and ability, relieved the monks of their burden by creating him Cardinal-Bishop of Albano.

The career of Nicholas Breakspear affords typical evidence of the scope offered to the most obscure Englishmen in the Middle Ages. The schools and the seats of learning being in the hands of the Church, they were open to the lowest and the poorest, an accessibility which they are only now, after four centuries, partially regaining. Secular rank was practically closed to all except those carrying right by birth; but promotion, power and authority in Church and State were open to all, whether rich or poor, noble or common. The peasant-born William of Wykeham in the fourteenth century became Bishop of Winchester and Chancellor of England by using the same opportunities as the royal Plantagenet, Henry Beaufort, who followed him. It is a point to be remembered when the servitude and autocracy of the Middle Ages is compared with the freedom and democracy of our own day.

Nicholas Breakspear, according to the scanty and uncertain records of his origins, was the son of a poor father, Robert Chambers, who later became a monk of S. Albans. According to one version Nicholas was rejected by the Abbot of S. Albans on the ground of incapacity, and according to another he was left without a protector when his father entered religion. For whatever cause, he is said to have begged his way to Paris, where he studied with distinction, and proceeded thence to Arles where he studied further, and thence again to the Convent of S. Rufus, where he became successively Prior and Abbot. It is equally probable, and certainly consonant with common practice, that he should have been helped to Paris by a patron, possibly the Abbot of S. Albans, because he showed early capability, his father entering the abbey much later. Whatever the truth of this matter, and there is no special authority for the more romantic version, Nicholas does not appear to have borne any ill-will towards the abbey which is reputed to have given him such a scurvy start in life. On the contrary he is said to have honoured it with a visit and the greatest good-will, after his journeys in Scandinavia, whither he was sent as papal legate. He is still honoured in Scandinavia as the ' Apostle of the North.'

After four years' missionary labours he returned to Rome and was unanimously elected Pope, taking the name of Adrian IV. He was enthroned on Christmas Day 1154.

In the same month Henry II suceeded to the English throne. There is no doubt as to which event caused the greater rejoicing amongst the people of England. Three English bishops, accompanied by John of Salisbury, the learned chronicler and former pupil of Robert Pullen, were sent to Rome to offer the English Pope the congratulations and homage of the English King and people. It was only Adrian who did not share in the general rejoicing. He told John that he missed the peace he had left in his cell at S. Rufus, and every step in greatness now increased his cares. To him the tiara was not so much a splendid as a burning crown.

After making all possible allowances for the customary eulogies of the great, it remains very

clear that the first and only English Cardinal to
sit in the Chair of S. Peter was a remarkably able
and holy man. The testimony of his contemporaries, with the single exception of the monks
of Canterbury, who were jealous of S. Albans, is
to the effect that he was a humble man, deeply
impressed by his office, kindly, learned and elo-
quent. He was famous as a preacher both for
the matter of his sermons and his resonant voice.

As Pope, Adrian proved himself a worthy up-
holder of the tradition of the great Hildebrand,
Gregory VII, in maintaining the dignity of the
Apostolic See. This brought him into conflict
with the most powerful of the Emperors, Frederick
the First, of the Red Beard. When they met to
discuss their differences the Emperor boldly
omitted the customary courtesy of holding the
Pope's stirrup for him, whereupon Adrian rode
away, until such time as the Emperor should learn
manners. Despite the military weakness of the
Papacy, and the uncertain extent of the papal
power, the Pope won and the Emperor knelt.
Though Adrian ultimately crowned Frederick he
had trouble with him again ; yet the Emperor was
able to effect nothing of serious weight against the
Holy See whilst the Englishman lived. When he
died, the Emperor supported an anti-pope in order
that he might divide and rule the Church, but he
was then too late.

As an example of the strong rule of Adrian IV may be cited his use of the weapon of the Interdict against the people of Rome itself. He laid the city under the ban to check the activities of the republican Arnold of Brescia after the murder of the Cardinal of S. Pudentiana, and the strong measure, dangerous though it was, succeeded completely.

A few months after Henry II's coronation John of Salisbury visited the English Pope with a petition for the papal approval of the invasion of Ireland, represented as a land of ignorant and vicious people fallen very far from the standard of sanctity set them by S. Patrick. Though the Pope must have seen through Henry's plea of wishing to carry enlightenment and faith to a barbarous people, being a much travelled and learned man he was doubtless aware of the condition of the Irish at this time, and all contemporary evidence goes to show that it was very bad indeed. England after the ruinous reign of Stephen was far from being a paradise, the people have perhaps never been so destitute and miserable, but the Irish under numerous warring chieftains, lacking any strong central government or authority, were in a far worse case. Moreover, the Church in Ireland had a somewhat uncertain connection with Rome, and successive missions, even the zeal of S. Malachy and the efforts of the Irish prelates, had been nullified by the turbulent state of the country.

The Pope saw in Henry's application a recognition of papal sovereignty, and granted the necessary approval, signifying his willingness that the King should enter Ireland and be acknowledged as ruler of the natives, *for the worthy ends which he had proposed*, exhorting him to bear always in mind the conditions on which the assent had been obtained. He could not know, in that day, what centuries of tyranny, brutality and oppression were to be inflicted upon the best of the Irish by the worst of the English. The Pope could hardly know what was even then splendid in the Irish character, still less what were its capabilities. He could hardly know the brutal savagery and uncontrolled passion of Henry, much less the rapacity of his successors, and the ignorant bigotry which a de-papalized religion was to give the English people. Henry had not yet mutilated the children of the Welsh nobles by gouging out the eyes of the males and cutting off the ears and noses of the females. The calamities of the future were mercifully, if unfortunately, hidden.

Henry did not, in fact, at once avail himself of the papal licence, but allowed Strongbow and other Welsh adventurers to ravage Ireland, taking over the conquered areas later. But from the time of Pope Adrian's licence or grant to Henry II,

Ireland knew no respite from England for seven hundred years.

The conflict between the King and the Church in England, between the personal authority of the King and the official authority of the Church, though foreshadowed in 1157, did not break out until after the death of the English Pope. In the matter of ecclesiastical appointments it is significant that Adrian is credited with being content to indicate his wishes rather than insisting on his own choice of candidates. There is no doubt, from his conception of the office of the Papacy and the nature of the Church, that he would have supported entirely, as did his successor Alexander III, the stand of S. Thomas à Becket against Henry on the matter of the ecclesiastical courts.

It is said, and it may well be true since Englishmen always honoured the Mother of God, that Pope Adrian wrote a treatise, *De Conceptione Virginis*.

At his death in 1159, he was buried with great pomp. At least two of his mortal enemies attended the funeral, not, so far as we know, from any other motive than respect.

III. BOSO BREAKSPEAR

Whilst Nicholas Breakspear was still Cardinal or possibly soon after he was made Pope, Boso

Breakspear was elevated to the Sacred College. Boso has been doubtfully described as a nephew of Nicholas on the maternal side. He was a Benedictine of the Abbey of S. Albans, and we may therefore safely accept the possibility that he was related to his namesake. This preference for nephews has for some obscure reason been stigmatized as a sort of ecclesiastical crime, though there is no *a priori* reason why a nephew whose character and ability, ancestry and training, are known should not be preferred to a stranger who is recommended by repute or the importunities of patrons or bribed agents. A pope, or for that matter any high officer in the Church, would be better advised to have about him men who are known to him and bound by some ties of indebtedness or relationship, than strangers of great merit and unknown behaviour. A nephew was moreover the nearest an ecclesiastic could decently get to his own kind. There is no doubt that a great deal of this preference for nephews, which becomes such a hideous offence when called by its Greek name of nepotism, though abused, was practically reasonable. 'The devil you know is better than the devil you don't know,' has on the whole proved a sound working principle.

In the case of Boso Breakspear no possible exception can be taken to his uncle's application of that principle. He had a wide and deserved reputation for piety and learning and was something of a *trouvère*. As Cardinal-deacon of SS. Cosmas and Damian he went on a mission to Portugal, and as papal delegate presided over the National Council at Burgos. He was an active supporter of Pope Alexander III against the anti-pope Victor, and when Alexander went to Venice to receive the submission of the Emperor Frederick, Boso went with him. He was later made Cardinal-priest of S. Pudentiana, thus preceding the present Cardinal-Archbishop of Westminster in that title. Although he does not appear to have had any direct connection with English affairs, his intimacy with Alexander III must have had considerable influence on English business in the papal court, especially in the matter of the King against S. Thomas à Becket. It is significant that Herbert of Bosham, faithful servant and chronicler of Becket, was made a Cardinal after the murder of the Archbishop. Hence for a considerable period there were two English Cardinals in a college of some two dozen, and since they would not be without English subordinates, England had in consequence very fair representation in the papal court.

Boso Breakspear's signature is attached to many bulls and papal documents during the pontificates of Adrian and Alexander. He is credited with several theological works, an account of Adrian's pontificate (long ago lost), and a continuation of the *Liber Pontificalis* from the death of Stephen V. This work, *Gesta Romanorum Pontificum*, was later published by Cencius Camerarius, afterwards Pope Honorius III, and it has formed the basis of many subsequent works. Perhaps his most interesting writings were nine poetical lives of women saints. At the end of the life of S. Agnes he adds a prayer for himself in his romance verse :

> ' *Jeo pri Agneis de Dieu cherie*
> *K'ele nus seit en aye*
> *E k'ele pri pur Bozun*
> *Ki ad descrit su passiun,*'

and to S. Mary Magdalene he prays :

> ' *Mais jeo pri Marie la dulce*
> *Ke sa bonte point ne grouce*
> *De ayder Bozun en son mester*
> *Ki sa vie vous translater*
> *Ki gent la pussent plus amer*
> *E del lire merit aver.*'

Bozun died about 1181.

IV.   HERBERT OF BOSHAM

There is some small doubt as to whether Herbert of Bosham, contemporary of Pullen, Boso Breakspear and Pope Adrian IV, was ever a Cardinal, though most authorities agree that he was. After the death of S. Thomas à Becket he appears to have become Archbishop of Benevento and

Cardinal under Pope Alexander III about 1178, or under Pope Lucius III a few years later. He is remembered chiefly for his attachment to S. Thomas, whose household he joined after a distinguished scholastic career in philosophy and theology in France and England. He was the closest and most faithful of S. Thomas's supporters, standing by him at Clarendon and at Northampton, whence they escaped together on one horse. He engineered the Archbishop's escape to the continent, suffered with him in exile and undertook none too safe missions on his behalf to the angry King. He stood by his master until the King's knights murdered the great priest in his Cathedral church. After that, presumably on the continent, he wrote the life of the Martyr and the *Liber Melorum* in praise of him.

It is said that King Henry taunted him with being a priest's son, and he replied that his father was not a priest until after he was born, which seems to indicate a situation similar to that of Nicholas Breakspear. We know nothing of Herbert of Bosham's activities as a Prince of the Church and he is not heard of after 1189.

V. STEPHEN LANGTON

From this point there was a break in English representation in the Sacred College until the elevation in 1206 of Stephen Langton as Cardinal-priest of S. Chrysogonus. Very little is known of this great priest's origins. By some he is said to have been a Yorkshireman, by others to have been born at Langton near Wragby, Lincolnshire, the son of Henry Langton, about 1165. By the time he appears on the stage of English history he is already Cardinal with a universal reputation for learning and uprightness.

He was chiefly famous as a philosopher, biblical scholar and preacher, being known on the continent as ' Stephen Linguatonans,' ' Stephen with the Tongue of Thunder.' At Paris, where he is said to have presided over the Schools (which were not yet a corporate University), he had achieved success as a biblical commentator, and his division of the Bible into chapters, remarkable for the fact that it applies to the Greek New Testament and the Septuagint equally, has been universally accepted even by the Eastern Churches and the Jews.

In 1205 died Archbishop Hubert Walter, another of the great ecclesiastics who, by undertaking the cares of State, preserved what stability was possible whilst the kings pillaged, raped, murdered and gnawed straw in the authentic Plantagenet manner. He had been an active and competent legislator both in Church and State, and had been especially careful of the rights of the

Church and fidelity to the Holy See as befitted a successor of S. Thomas. He was responsible for special emphasis on devotion to the Blessed Sacrament.

England being now under King John, not only the worst of his line but probably the worst of all kings of England (though it is dangerous to speak with confidence where this honour has been so keenly contested), it was all the more necessary that the leading figure of the greater Power should be a good man. The hour found the man, but the King instinctively rejected him. The monks of Christ Church, Canterbury, with whom the election lay, chose their sub-prior Reginald, without asking for the customary royal *congé d'élire*, and packed him off to Rome for papal confirmation. The bishops of the Province, considering that they should have some say in the choice of so important a dignitary, sent a deputation of protest to Rome. John made the bishops withdraw their claim to interfere, and ordered the monks to elect canonically John de Gray, Bishop of Norwich. As the King's favourite, we need not inquire further into the demerits of the Bishop of Norwich. The monks obeyed John. The Pope, on the report of a commission sent to examine the monks, declared both elections void. He gave a mandate to the monks in Rome to elect yet another, and named Stephen Langton, Cardinal-priest of

S. Chrysogonus.   So the monks of Christ Church
made their third choice.   King John, however, did
not.   He refused to allow the new Archbishop into
the country, and it was six years before the power
of the Pope overcame the obstinacy of the King
and the Cardinal was able to take possession of
the primatial see.

The problem of election to the Archbishopric
of Canterbury was by no means the simple matter
some historians, especially those favourable to the
papal claims, have concluded.   The monks of
Christ Church had a clear traditional right, respected by successive sovereigns, from the time
of the first Archbishop, S. Augustine.   But their
disadvantage is obvious.   Their exclusion from
the world may not have been so complete as might
be rashly assumed ; the records of monastic chroniclers show that they knew a good deal of what
was going on, yet their errors show that they
were often badly informed.   They were indeed
competent enough to choose their own superior,
but in the case of Christ Church that superior
automatically became very much more.   He became a figure of first importance in the affairs of
the State, ecclesiastical and civil.   So far as the
Church was concerned, it was necessary that
the Pope should have some say in the matter ; the
bishops of the Province being directly affected in
themselves and their flocks, ought to be con-

sidered ; the King, since Church and State were so closely knit, could not reasonably be denied a voice.

Pope, Bishops and King were clearly in a better position to find the man than were the monks. Pope and King, who had most power in the matter, were both liable, and usually given, to personal prejudice. In the long run the appointment rested, in effect, with the Pope as the most powerful ; and so long as he did not intrude a foreigner, he was most likely to make a sound choice. He was in the best position to be advised. His immediate personal interest was normally less than that of the King. Though the corruption of this our mortality made no distinction of persons, it undoubtedly flourished more freely, though not necessarily more vigorously, in royal courts.

In the present case, the Pope was able to insist on the appointment of a strong, upright Englishman to the chair of S. Augustine.

Cardinal Stephen Langton was consecrated Archbishop by the Pope at Viterbo. The angry King drove the monks from Christ Church and defied the Pope. Innocent laid England under an Interdict, a severe measure in which, curiously enough, the King alone is exempt whilst his subjects suffer. The position of the King, even in the days of absolute monarchs, feudal tyrants and merciless rulers, depended so much on the people,

that this weapon was one of the most powerful
the Papacy had against defiant princes, and it very
rarely failed.   It deprived everybody, except the
King, infants and the dying, of the Sacraments
and the ministrations of the clergy.   Churches
were closed, and the dead were buried without
ceremony in unconsecrated ground.

John thought, as many might think now, that
he could ignore all this. He forbade the publication of the ban and drove into exile the three
bishops instructed to publish it. He maltreated
and imprisoned their relatives and threatened the
clergy generally. Repenting of this rashness he
ordered that anyone, except himself, who molested
the clergy, should be hanged, if they were caught,
on the nearest oak : '*Si quem attingere possumus,
ad proximum quercum eum suspendi faciemus.*'

The interdict lasted nearly six years. Meanwhile John went on the war-path against the Scots,
Irish and Welsh, ravaging, despoiling and hanging
hostages in his royal way. At the end of the first
year the Pope excommunicated him. Since the
next step would be deposition and invasion for
the purpose of forcible dethronement, John began
to collect foreign allies and levies. After four
years came the papal deposition—releasing the
King's vassals from their oaths and calling upon
faithful Christian princes to depose him forcibly
and enthrone a loyal son of the Church. The

King of France, being the readiest for the purpose, prepared to act. John reopened negotiations —he was a very obvious coward—but since he was also a well-attested liar and perjurer who could not be trusted, the Pope sent his envoy Pandulph to receive his formal submission.

In that submission the King ' granted, *not through fear of force but of his own free will*, to God, to the holy apostles Peter and Paul, to Pope Innocent and Innocent's rightful successors, the kingdom of England and the kingdom of Ireland, to be holden by himself and his heirs in body of the Bishop of Rome in fee, by the annual rent of one thousand marks.' He swore fealty to the Pope as a vassal to his lord. He did not add that he had done this from a superstitious fear of the prophecy of Peter the Hermit, who said that by the feast of the Ascension he would cease to reign. The prophecy being fulfilled (for he was now no longer a sovereign but a vassal) he hanged the Hermit for a false prophet.

The reconcilement between Innocent and John pleased everybody except the King of France, who was thus baulked of a new territory. John was under an obligation to restore the seized property of the clergy and to allow the exiles to return. Never being in a hurry to keep his word he tried first to attack the withdrawing French, but his barons, who had already suffered as much of John

c

as they could stand, saw their opportunity and refused to support him. He was still under the ban of excommunication. To clear himself he invited the exiles to return and sent them conduct money.

The Cardinal-Archbishop with several bishops and the monks of Christ Church, met the King at Winchester, and almost too precipitately revoked the sentence of excommunication. The King made another attempt to carry war to France, but when he got to Jersey he found that none had followed him. The barons had followed the Cardinal, who had lost no time in stiffening their opposition to the King, and bound them by an oath to defend their liberties against him. John, foaming at the mouth, threatened wholesale executions. At Northampton and again at Nottingham he was reminded by the Cardinal that the accused had the right to be tried by their peers. Langton finally brought the King to reason and stopped his warfare by threatening to excommunicate all his supporters.

The Pope now sent a legate to arbitrate on the extent of the compensation to be made by the King, and to lift the interdict when that was settled. The King, whose dissimulation may have deceived the papal legate, though it was well known to his barons and Langton, agreed heartily to anything in order to regain the support of Innocent.

The interdict was removed after he had returned to France to carry on the war. At Bouvines John, with greatly superior numerical forces, suffered a crushing defeat. He negotiated for peace through Cardinal Robert Curzon, or de Courçon, an Englishman said to be a native of Kedleston in Derbyshire, now *legate a latere* to the French court. John gained a five years' truce, on such terms that the French were probably right when they said that Cardinal Curzon acted ' as one Englishman for another.'

John Lackland now came back to England. He was naturally alarmed that no one appeared to take much notice of his return, and his court was strangely bare of barons. He is said to have shut himself up in the Temple, London. It was in London a few days later that he was presented with a formidable list of demands by the barons. Finding the high hand ineffective he played for time, and promised an answer by Easter on the security of the Cardinal-Archbishop and others. Evidently the Cardinal was no longer formally and openly leading the barons. His design of consolidating them was now completed.

The King proceeded to garrison castles, send abroad for mercenaries, and bribe the clergy to the extent of conceding a few of their first demands. To secure himself further he took the Cross, for by so doing he would gain the protection and privileges accorded by the Church to Crusaders.

Both the King and his opponents had sent appeals to Rome to gain papal support. The barons expected some assistance out of gratitude for their former withstanding of the King. Innocent, however, now considered it politic to support the weaker side, his vassal the King, and wrote to the Cardinal-Archbishop on the King's behalf, mentioned that there was more than a suspicion that the Cardinal himself had encouraged the opposition, and ordered him to work for a peaceful settlement. To the barons the Pope wrote reprovingly for demanding what they should ask as a favour. They had no business to demand anything in the way of rights and liberties from his vassal the King except through him. This was all part of Innocent's policy, *divide et impera*.

From Oxford at Easter 1215, John sent the Cardinal-Archbishop, now an intermediary, and others, to ascertain the demands of the barons and knights assembled at Brackley. He brought back what was in effect the Magna Carta. The King had seen this before, at the Temple a few months ago, and did not like it. He told his commissioners to appeal to the Pope, offer to abolish certain objectionable customs and take advice about others. But the barons knew their man and declined to consider his evasions. Pandulph, the papal legate, and Simon, Bishop of Exeter, argued that Langton should, in obedience to the Pope, excommunicate the refractory barons and their supporters. The Cardinal replied that he knew the intentions of the Pope better (though it is doubtful whether this was true), and he was more inclined to lay the ban on the King's foreign levies. The King, inveterate shuffler, suggested referring the dispute to four nominees of the barons, four of his own and the Pope. The barons wisely declined. Instead of further parley, they marched against him, eventually occupying London.

As usual whenever he was faced with strength, John quailed. He offered to yield and suggested a conference. He met the barons at Runnymede, supported, outwardly at least, by eight bishops and fifteen others, with the nobility of the country ranged against him. He signed the Great Charter, without much intention of honouring his signature. Its clauses, valuable though they were as a check to the despotism of bad kings and a safeguard to the rights of freemen and the nobility, especially the nobility, declined in importance with the feudal system. They were designed by Cardinal Langton primarily against the abuses in that system, and not, as is often fondly supposed, as a basis of liberty for the citizens of a democracy. Yet they operated, indirectly, and in a small measure, to that end.

John, as was expected, broke his word readily enough. But the Charter served its purpose and was a permanent defence against the monarchy, though it needed thirty-eight ratifications more by seven successive kings. In all these final negotiations with John, Stephen Langton was outwardly impartial. He had already done what was necessary.

Following Runnymede, John began to provision and fortify his castles. When the barons expressed their suspicions he assured them that the provisions of the Charter were being put into operation, but he first required signed charters of fealty to himself. They refused. The Cardinal was now once more finding it necessary to side against the King, who continued to bring over hordes of mercenaries.

Eventually there came from Pope Innocent to the King an annulment of the Great Charter and a condemnation of the violence of the barons on the grounds already mentioned. He exhorted the barons to submit themselves and their case before a council in Rome. Finding them obdurate he instructed the Cardinal-Primate to excommunicate them. It must have been something of a shock to the Pope, and a surprise even to John, when Langton refused. No doubt he justified his refusal, as he did his former conduct and the barons did theirs, on the grounds that the Pope was being misled by John.

The Pope could hardly do less than suspend
Langton from the exercise of his archiepiscopal
office. Though he attended the council at Rome
he could not move the Pope in his favour again.
Innocent excommunicated the leading barons and
laid an interdict upon London. Meanwhile John
ravaged the country with fire and sword and let
his foreign levies loose to plunder his miserable
subjects. Louis, son of the French King Philip,
stepped in with an army and occupied London,
where he was received as King and great numbers
acclaimed him. Alexander of Scotland marched
from Carlisle to Dover, under John's nose, to do
homage to Louis. Soon after this, John lost
his crown, as everybody knows, in the Wash,
and died a miserable death amid general rejoicing.

The accession of the young son of John, Henry
of Winchester, reconciled some barons and the
people to their monarch. Louis, who had out-
lived his welcome, was eventually driven out,
though partly bought out.

The Cardinal-Archbishop of Canterbury, now
allowed to resume his functions, could leave affairs
to take their course under the barons who rallied
round the boy Henry III and Pope Honorius III
who had succeeded Innocent. He confined himself henceforth to the rehabilitation of the ravaged
Church in his Province. In April 1222 he opened

a council at Osney which was to the Church what Runnymede was to the State. At this synod was promulgated a code of discipline of forty-two canons for the government of the See of Canterbury.

Well might the chronicler Capgrave record : ' In XI yere of Henry deied Stevene Langdon that was a grete clerk in his daye.' There have been very few greater.

The famous Dr. Martin Farquhar Tupper, Fellow of the Royal Society in the early nineteenth century, based a novel on his life. It sold in tens of thousands and sells to-day, a masterpiece of pompous erudite ignorance combined with a pleasing banality and bigotry which make it one of the finest pieces of unconscious humour in our language. If we ask why the Cardinal of S. Chrysogonus was thus chosen for hero, our answer is in the fact that he resisted the Pope's patronage of John, and therefore, in the words of Dr. Tupper, ' long antedated Luther.'

VI. Robert Curzon

Robert Curzon, whose name is spelt variously Curson, de Courçon, de Corceone and de Curchun, was born at Kedleston, Derbyshire, of a noble, that is Norman, family. He probably studied at Oxford, certainly at Paris where he distinguished himself, and Rome. In 1204 he was Canon of Noyon and in 1211 Canon of Paris. He was responsible for incorporating the schools of Paris as a university by the charter he gained from Pope Innocent III in 1211, and it is said that he became Chancellor of the University on that occasion. In 1212 or 1213 he was created Cardinal-priest of S. Stefano in Monte Celio and very soon afterwards *legate a latere* to the French court. It is therefore most improbable that he could have been legate to England before this, as some authorities have assumed. He presided over a commission to enquire into abuses, ecclesiastical and academical, at Paris, and his particular denunciation of usury on this occasion was later quoted, amongst other 'fathers and doctors,' by Robert Grosseteste, Bishop of Lincoln. Without much direct evidence he has been credited with a certain amount of double dealing—the French did not like the way he negotiated the truce between Philip of France and John of England after Bouvines, as we have already observed.

As legate he was charged to preach a Crusade, and in doing so he is said to have denounced the clergy to please the people, but since the accusation is made in clerical records, we may allow the possibility that he denounced the clergy because they deserved it. Nevertheless his action, after deposing the Abbot of S. Martial at Limoges, in appointing a successor who offered him half the treasure of the abbey for himself, was at least suspicious. Yet again we have no evidence that he accepted the bribe.

He certainly appears to have held his position by his abilities and character rather than by any personal popularity or virtue. Whilst he was preaching the Crusade against the Albigensians, in which he took the cross himself, the people of Cahors were in trouble for shutting him out of the town, and in 1216 we find him rebuked by Pope Innocent III for being at loggerheads with the clergy again. Just before this he had achieved a diplomatic settlement of a dispute between the Chancellor and the University of Paris and drawn up regulations for the government of the University.

Cardinal Curzon enjoyed the confidence of Pope Honorius, who succeeded Innocent. He was not so much a pious as a learned and able prelate, with perhaps more of the ruler than the priest in his character. He would naturally figure very prominently at the Lateran Council in 1215. He finally went on the Crusade and died at the siege of Damietta in 1218.

VII. ROBERT SOMERCOTE

For another twenty years we do not find an English representative in the Sacred College. We hear of Cardinal Langton's conferring the benefices of Caister, Norfolk and Croydon on Robert Somercote. In 1238 we find the same Somercote created Cardinal of S. Eustachius by Pope Gregory IX, to whom he was closely attached. He had been for some time at the papal court with his brother Lawrence, and both had been sub-deacons to the Pope.

Robert Somercote is said to have always remembered that he was an Englishman, and furthered English suits at Rome. Matthew Paris, the chronicler of S. Albans, who was writing at this very time, says he was the most eminent of all the Cardinals. It is recorded as certain that, had he not died during the consistory to elect a successor to Gregory IX (on September 26, 1241), he would have been elected himself, and thus become the second English Pope. He was buried in the Basilica of S. Chrysogonus, and his close friend Godfrey of Milan became for a brief space Celestine IV. He had been distinguished for his learning and prudence and had provided valuable help to the Pope against the mighty Frederick II, Stupor Mundi. There is no doubt that the history of

Europe would have taken a very different turn had this Englishman succeeded to carry on the fight against the Emperor.

VIII. JOHN OF TOLEDO

In 1244 Pope Innocent IV created Cardinal of S. Lorenzo in Lucina, a Cistercian of Toledo, named John. He is referred to by a Spanish authority as John the Englishman, and the chronicler Matthew of Westminster says he was a monk remarkable for his accomplishments and scholarship, and that he remonstrated with the Pope about papal extortions in England. He had apparently studied at Toledo and entered the Cistercian Convent, remaining there until he was created Cardinal. He attended Innocent IV on his wanderings when that Pope fled from his one-time friend Frederick II. He assisted at the election of Urban IV, and it is said that when Urban's successor, Clement IV, died in 1268, John of Toledo was a favourite for the Papacy, but being English he was defeated owing to his unpopularity with the Italians. John continued to serve the Papacy actively until his death in 1214 during the Council of Lyons, having been a Cardinal for thirty years, under five Popes. He founded a monastery at Viterbo.

IX. Hugh of Evesham

One other English Cardinal of this period, Hugh of Evesham, was more concerned with the papal court than with England. From the end of the twelfth century until the suppression of the Faith in England, most of the English Cardinals will be found to remain in office in their own country. Hugh of Evesham was educated at Oxford and Cambridge and also in France and Italy, being nicknamed Lenoir, Il Nero, and by Latin writers Atratus, from which we may safely conclude that he looked black. Later he was known as ' Phœnix ' (the bird we see on his arms). He gained a great name as a mathematician and physician, being, according to some authorities, private physician to Pope Martin IV, who invited him to Rome.

Whilst at the papal court Hugh acted as proctor for the Archbishop of York, and correspondence shows that he was an old schoolfellow of Archbishop Peckham of Canterbury. He was created Cardinal of S. Lorenzo in Lucina by Martin IV at Orvieto on March 23, 1281. He held many benefices in England, being Archdeacon of Worcester and Prebendary of York, with several livings in that diocese. He died in Rome on July 27, 1287, some have said by poison, but there is no confirmation of the rumour. Pope Honorius IV showed his esteem by erecting a fine monument to his memory. Hugh of Evesham's works include *De Genealogis humanis, Canones medicales, Problemata*, and a Sermon for Septuagesima Sunday, of which there is a manuscript in the Bodleian Library.

It would seem that Englishmen in the thirteenth century were well to the fore in medical science. Some thirty or forty years before Cardinal Hugh, there had been a distinguished English physician at the court of Gregory IX, Richard of Wendover, who was Canon of S. Paul's, London.

X. DOUBTFUL

Several doubtful Cardinals are mentioned in various places as having been created before the end of the twelfth century. John Cummin, said to have been Archbishop of Dublin and, according to Giraldus Cambrensis, built the metropolitan church, is given as Cardinal-priest, created in 1183. Acherus, said to have been an Englishman, created in 1261 and died in 1286 ; William Bray, created in 1262 and died in 1282 ; Berardus is given in Godwin's *Præsulibus* as an English Cardinal created in 1288, died 1291. Theobald Stampendis, a distinguished teacher at Oxford, said to have written a book against the regular clergy dedicated to Archbishop Thurstan, is also said to have been created Cardinal by Innocent II, but he was probably legate only. Others named are Thomas Anglus, John Thoresby, Gremoaldus, and Sartorius Wallensis.

CHAPTER II

THE SCHOOLMEN

COMMENCING with the reign of Edward I, and the rise of the Dominican Order, the English Cardinals generally ceased to be particularly active at the papal court and in European affairs. The next four or five at least were Cardinals for a brief space only. More of them are now found at home, filling the Primacy and taking the lead in ecclesiastical government or as scholars and theologians. All of them begin as scholars even if they end as prelates, statesmen and administrators.

The English Constitution owes more to Primates, and especially those who were also Cardinals from Langton onwards, than to any other class of men. Their work is not to be measured by the noise they have left behind.

I. ROBERT KILWARDBY

One of the greatest of these Primates, and one of the most distinguished of all the English Cardinals in the Middle Ages, was Robert Kilwardby, the first friar to become Archbishop of Canterbury, in 1272, being the Pope's personal choice to settle that common difficulty—a deadlock between the King and the chapter of Christ Church, Canterbury. The Pope was Gregory X, who, as Archdeacon of Liège, had accompanied Henry III's son Edward on a Crusade, and it is therefore improbable that there was any serious difference between him and the new King Edward I on the choice of the Primate.

At Paris Kilwardby had been famous as a grammarian before he became a religious. Paris about that time (1252–9) held the greatest of all the schoolmen, Thomas Aquinas, and no doubt the eminence given by him and his master Albert to the Order of Preachers attracted Kilwardby. He joined the Order and achieved great distinction as a logician, being foremost in developing the doctrine of the syllogism. He made excellent abridgements of Aristotle and edited the works of S. Augustine. He is credited with thirty-nine philosophical treatises, his most important work being *De ortu Scientiarum*—' on the origin of the sciences.' Of his theological works his commentaries on the scriptures and Fathers, his treatises *de Passione Christi* and *de Sacramento altaris*, were the most widely known.

As provincial of the English Dominicans he is said to have founded their house Blackfriars in

D

London. He was a vigorous and strong disciplinarian, attending in person at Oxford to condemn errors in grammar, logic and natural philosophy. He is mentioned as being active in the cause of S. Richard of Chichester who was canonized in 1262.

In 1278 Pope Nicholas III created Robert Kilwardby Cardinal-Bishop of Porto and S. Rufina. When he went to Rome he resigned the Archbishopric, but took with him the registers and judicial records of the See of Canterbury, so that none remain of earlier date than his successor Peckham. As the resignation was made to the Pope by whom he had been selected for election, the Pope nominated his successor, and no request was made to the King respecting the temporalities. Since this omission appeared to carry the presumption that the temporalities were in the gift of the Pope, the King objected, but he appears to have been satisfied with the explanation that the omission was a clerk's error, and the Pope by setting up this excuse admitted that the temporals were the King's. This matter provided a constant bone of contention which was to appear again later under Edward III. The Cardinal died at Viterbo on joining the Curia, eighteen months after his elevation. Later historians have suggested that he was poisoned, but Nicholas Trivet, a contemporary chronicler, gives no hint of such a thing. More probably he had ended his normal span, for he was a fairly old man, perhaps seventy-five, when he died.

II. WILLIAM MACCLESFIELD

Hardly less famous in his day was the next English Cardinal, William Macclesfield, also a Dominican, one of the most renowned of the medieval Dominican theologians and a great scriptural scholar. He was, naturally enough, a zealous disciple of S. Thomas Aquinas at Paris, and took his doctorate at Oxford. He defended the papal teaching against Henry of Ghent and William de la Mare, and it is said that his work against the latter still survives. He preached a famous sermon before the English clergy on the discipline of the Church.

Macclesfield attended several Chapters-General of his Order and was a close friend of Pope Benedict XI, also a Dominican, who created him Cardinal-priest of S. Sabina on December 18, 1303. He died either during the celebrations in honour of his elevation or before the news reached him. Some say that the Pope conferred the honour ' not knowing that he was already dead,' which if it were true might reasonably exclude him from the line of English Cardinals, but Trivet, contemporary of Macclesfield, says he died before the news reached him. The Pope immediately replaced him in the title, on February 21, 1304, by another English Dominican, Walter Winterbourne.

Macclesfield's fame was sufficient to gain him the title of Doctor Inclytus, the Illustrious Doctor, amongst the scholars of Europe. He was buried in Blackfriars, London, and the insignia of his Cardinalate was placed on his tomb.

III. Walter Winterbourne

Walter Winterbourne, the third in this succession of English Dominican Cardinals, was born in the neighbourhood of Old Sarum. He was educated at Oxford and took his doctorate either there or at Paris. Many works of reference, repeating one another in the usual manner, assert that he was Provincial of the English Dominicans, but he was not. He directly affected English history perhaps a little more than his fellows, since he was remembrancer and later confessor and spiritual director to Edward I—at the time when that monarch invaded Scotland whence he had stolen the coronation stone now in Westminster.

It is said, and it is neither unlikely nor unreasonable, that Winterbourne used his influence to secure posts for his servants, and benefices and pardons for his friends. Fuller, in his *Worthies*, says of him that he was in his youth a good poet and orator, in middle age an acute philosopher, and in old age a deep controversial divine and a skilful casuist. Trivet, who was his friend, wrote of him generously as a friend might, and said that he was endowed with superb qualities, natural and supernatural, thoroughly versed in knowledge and graced with rare modesty and a kindly disposition, a model of religious piety and erudition. Without these testimonials, however, he was chosen by a fellow-Dominican, Pope Benedict XI, to take up the Cardinalate so speedily vacated by William Macclesfield. Although himself only Cardinal for a short time he assisted at the election of Pope Clement V, who achieved the distinction of being put into Dante's Hell.

Cardinal Winterbourne died on his way to join the new Pope at Lyons in the late summer of 1305. He was buried in the Dominican Church at Genoa by the Cardinal-Bishop of Ostia. The rumour that his remains were transferred to Blackfriars, London, may be due to confusing him with his predecessor Macclesfield. He left many sermons, commentaries and theological dissertations, but none is known to have survived.

IV. THOMAS JOYCE

The fourth and last of this unique succession
of Dominican Cardinals was Thomas Joyce or Jorz,
a Londoner, and one of six brothers, all Dominicans, and two of them successively Archbishops
of Armagh. He had the distinction, probably
shared by his fellows Macclesfield and Winterbourne, of studying at Paris in the heyday of
S. Thomas Aquinas, the Angelic Doctor, and
Albertus Magnus. He may have sat as a student
under both Albert and S. Thomas. As doctor of
theology he taught at Paris, Oxford and London,
eventually becoming Prior of the Dominicans at
Oxford and Provincial of the English Province.
He followed Walter Winterbourne as confessor to
Edward I and then as Cardinal-priest of S. Sabina,
being the third English Dominican in succession
in that title. This honour came to him, apparently,
after he had been sent by King Edward on a mission to Pope Clement V at Lyons, no doubt principally on the matter of sovereignty over Scotland,
where the King was then routing Wallace and
Bruce.

After his elevation to the Sacred College,
Thomas Joyce spent the remaining five years of
his life at the papal court. It was soon after he
joined the Curia that Edward wrote him to urge

the canonization of the great Grosseteste, Bishop
of Lincoln, a mission in which he unfortunately
failed. He played an important rôle during his
few years in the Curia. He was appointed to hear
the evidence against Pope Boniface VIII, brought
by Philip IV of France, and he was one of the
judges in the dispute on the poverty of the Franciscans. It may well have been in this connection
that he wrote his tract *De paupertate Christi*—
' on the poverty of Christ.' He died at Grenoble
in 1310 on a papal mission to the Emperor Henry
VII, and he was finally buried in the church at
Oxford where he had been Prior. His many
works include *Liber de beata visione*—' a Book of
Beatific Vision,' and *De Conceptione virginis*—
' on the Conception of the Virgin.' This last is
doubtful, but, knowing the English predilection
for the subject, it is probable.

His concise and effective refutation of the
attacks of Duns Scotus, the Subtle Doctor, on
the teaching of S. Thomas still enjoys considerable
repute. It forms the first book of his *Commentaria
in IV libros Sententiarum*.

V. SIMON LANGHAM

The succession of Dominican Cardinals, evidence of the influence of the Order at the papal

court and its success at this time, was a natural result of the great increase in status given to it by Albertus Magnus and his pupil S. Thomas. The Order had flourished at Oxford, and Oxford with it, as never before. That University, largely owing to the influence of the friars, now stood as high as any seat of learning in Europe, with the possible exception of Paris. England had produced Schoolmen who could hold their own with the greatest in disputations and in the exposition of scripture, canon law and theology. The group of Dominican Cardinals gives a fair measure of the standard of English scholarship in the days of the great scholars, the end of the thirteenth century, when medieval culture was at the peak. Naturally enough the heights achieved by S. Thomas were not easily scaled or easy to hold. There was an inevitable decline. It was part of the general decline in medieval civilization which preceded the Renaissance. Not only in the realm of learning but elsewhere the medievals found it hard to maintain the high standard of achievement set up by the giants of the thirteenth century. It was difficult for any Pope to follow Innocent III as it was difficult for any Emperor to follow Frederick II, and in a lesser way it was too much for Edward II to follow Edward I, though he did not try very hard.

The decline was not necessarily so serious or

extensive as many have liked to suppose, but the period succeeding the peak of the Middle Ages suffers by the contrast. The difficulties of the Papacy in the migration to Avignon were reflected throughout the Church. The seats of learning, being essentially ecclesiastical, were bound to suffer in consequence. So far as England was concerned what the Universities lost in scope they gained in local importance and material extension through the foundation and endowment of colleges by the great churchmen of the fourteenth century, such as William of Wykeham. From the end of the thirteenth century we find the greatest English ecclesiastics more closely concerned with home affairs than papal. They held high office in the State as well as in the Curia or at the seats of learning, and we find the Cardinals, though still great scholars, since their scholastic record was as a rule the first thing to give them distinction and gain them preferment, now exercising a direct influence on English government as Ministers of the Crown. Hitherto few, except Stephen Langton, have been prominent as statesmen ; all have been eminent scholars. Henceforth, until the Revolt, most of them will be statesmen. We may observe at this juncture that whereas the English Cardinals have so far been men of good character, we shall find them, during the next two and a half centuries, somewhat the worse for contact with the affairs of State. The political atmosphere has never been healthy for the morals.

Under Edward III England rose to unprecedented eminence in Europe. Edward I had gained a reputation as a leader of chivalry. His son Edward II had done nothing to maintain it, but his grandson, the third Edward, fully compensated for his father's defection, and with the aid of his son, the Black Prince, made English chivalry the admiration of Europe. The Order of the Garter was founded in the middle of the fourteenth century. We won a great naval victory at Sluys. The Black Prince fought and won Crecy and Poitiers, adding most of France to the English possessions. The Kings of France and Scotland were prisoners in England.

Thus it was that the King of England was in no particular mood to suffer interference in temporal matters from a Pope who had lost much of his temporal power and was more or less in exile and bondage at Avignon. In 1351 was enacted the Statute of Provisors, against the provision by the Pope of his nominees, especially foreigners, to English bishoprics and other benefices. Later in the same reign was enacted the Statute of Praemunire against appeals to the jurisdiction of the papal courts. Both these acts of a strong King against a weak Pope were done to prevent en-

croachments on the power of the King in the
temporal concerns of the Church in his dominion.
They were in no sense Protestant or anti-papal, or
properly an example of the resistance of Englishmen to papal authority. The spiritual jurisdiction
of the Pope and his authority in doctrinal matters
was clearly acknowledged and never questioned by
these acts. Thus it was that the acts were made
and confirmed under the administration and with
the approval of such great ecclesiastics as Simon
Langham and William of Wykeham.

Simon Langham was a Benedictine of the Abbey
of Westminster. He was born at Langham in
Rutlandshire and entered the Abbey about 1335.
He became successively Prior and Abbot by 1349.
He was probably the greatest Abbot Westminster
ever had, and came to be known as its second
founder. He reformed the discipline of the Abbey
and completed a good deal of building, including
the cloisters. In 1360 he was made Treasurer of
England, in 1362 Bishop of Ely—he had been
elected to the Bishopric of London, but wisely
chose Ely. He was made Chancellor of England
in 1363, and is said, with scant authority, to have
been the first chancellor to address Parliament in
English. There is more reason to believe that this
distinction is to the credit of a greater though
less famous bishop and chancellor, William of
Wykeham. During this period of office the Statute

of Praemunire was reaffirmed. In this Langham appears to have acquiesced, and in addition to have strongly opposed pluralism, which had been encouraged both by Pope and King. The King especially found it useful to reward his servants with a plurality of benefices and the Popes had done the same thing. Nevertheless at this time both found it necessary, for motives of their own, to pronounce against them. Yet there were various and many methods of evasion, and Bishop and Chancellor Langham was glad to put a check on the practice. It was not, however, at that period the grave crime that recent historians have been inclined to assume. The holders of many benefices rarely neglected their cures entirely, but provided deputies, though sometimes at sweated rates, and many pluralists took over with their benefices the responsibility for church property which in England at least would otherwise have suffered neglect and deterioration, owing to the serious shortage of priests after the Great Plague.

In 1366 Langham was made Archbishop of Canterbury. Two years later he was created Cardinal-priest of S. Sixtus by B. Urban V, to the great annoyance of King Edward III, who saw in this act an attempt to rob him of his most able chancellor and so handicap him in his conflict over the papal claims. Langham, loyal as he was to the King, obeyed his spiritual lord the Pope, accepted the Cardinal's Hat, and resigned the Archbishopric of Canterbury.

Before he resigned he removed John Wyclif from the wardenship of Canterbury Hall, Oxford, a position to which he had been misled into appointing that turbulent priest. His last act as Archbishop was to order prayers against the plague and grant forty days' indulgence to those attending the intercessory processions ' trusting in the mercy of Almighty God and the merits and prayers of the Blessed Virgin Mary his Mother, holy Thomas the glorious martyr, and all the saints.'

Whether he was personally more needed or appreciated by the King, he was not long out of favour. Edward III was too good a king and too just a man to lose a good servant through pique. At this time he needed support against the Pope, and if he could not get support he might at least decrease opposition by keeping friendly with his ex-chancellor.

In 1373 Pope Gregory XI created Simon Cardinal-Bishop of Palestrina, and refused to release him when in the following year he was again elected Archbishop of Canterbury.

When Cardinal Langham died at Avignon in 1396 he left a fortune not far short of the equivalent of a quarter of a million pounds in modern money. It may be, as some biographers assert, that he came of a rich family, though it is difficult to imagine any comparatively unknown family in the days of his youth being very rich, especially after the reigns of the kings who had devastated the country in the wars against the barons. It is hardly likely that many of the nobility in those hectic days accumulated much actual wealth. The Church was rich and protected, to a large extent, by its sacred character. We may safely conclude that Simon Langham's great administrative ability had not deserted him when it came to his own financial affairs. He bequeathed most of his fortune to the Abbey of Westminster, whither his body was brought in 1379, three years after his death. His tomb, one of the finest in the Abbey, is in S. Benet's Chapel and forms a pleasing contrast to the marble furniture erected to the memory of statesmen of a later age. He was not only a great man, but a good one, described by contemporary chroniclers as courteous and kindhearted.

VI. ADAM EASTON

The creation of Adam Easton as Cardinal-priest of S. Cecilia by Pope Urban VI, five years after the death of Cardinal Simon Langham, affords a further example of the equality of opportunity for rich and poor which existed in medieval England

The advocates of compulsory free education have often tried to justify the modern system on the ground that it provides this equality of opportunity, presumably for the first time. Education in the scholastic sense was accessible to all who desired it and showed an aptitude for it in the Middle Ages.

Wykeham, a peasant's son, rose to be the founder of Winchester School and New College, the College of Blessed Mary at Oxford, these being the basis of the Public School and University collegiate system. Certainly scholarship was not then wasted on those who had neither inclination nor aptitude for it and would never appreciate it. They were left to learn their trade or craft and become useful productive citizens. They were every bit as educated as the average citizen of to-day, and they were on the whole less gullible because they could not read, and printing was not yet invented for their confusion. For those who wanted, like Adam Easton, to read and write, the way was open.

Easton was a poor man's son, born near Norwich. After sufficient preliminary education he became a Benedictine. At Oxford he graduated doctor in theology and became famous for his Hebrew and Greek scholarship, this, be it noted, long before the Renaissance. His name first appears publicly as a witness against one John

Wyclif, who was appealing against dismissal from the wardenship of Canterbury Hall, Oxford, which dismissal was, as we have observed already, the act of Simon Langham, Archbishop of Canterbury.

It is not unlikely that Adam Easton went to Rome with Langham ; they were both Benedictines. He is evidently well established at the papal court (now back at Rome) by the time Cardinal Langham dies. Soon after his elevation to the Sacred College with the title of Cardinal-priest of S. Cecilia, he was preferred by papal provision (so much for the Statute of Provisors) to the Deanery of York. He has been referred to in various works, dated as early as the beginning of the seventeenth century, as Bishop of London, but there is no evidence for this. It is more probable that he went abroad soon after he is first heard of and remained there.

On the accusation that he was concerned with five other Cardinals in a conspiracy against his former patron Urban VI, he was imprisoned with them at Nocera in 1385, where he spent a literally torturous time in a most unpleasant dungeon. Urban VI was not the kindest of men. When he was driven from Nocera he killed Easton's five fellow-Cardinals and conspirators, but apparently spared the Englishman on account of the importunities of Richard II. Easton was deprived of his English benefices and Cardinalate and sent away in custody to spend the rest of his life as ' a poor monk,' which, considering his experiences, should have been no great hardship.

When Urban died the poor English monk's reputation was still sufficient to induce the new Pope, Boniface IX, to restore him to his former dignity, in 1389. He obtained the English benefice of Yetminster Secunda, a prebend of Salisbury, and revisited England, no doubt on business between the Pope and Richard II, for the King's intervention on his behalf suggests strongly that he represented English interests in the Curia. England had supported Urban against the French anti-pope known as Clement VII, yet the question of papal provision to English benefices had frequently arisen and was usually dealt with by a reaffirmation of the Statutes of Provisors and Praemunire. Urban, with France against him, could not afford to lose English support. Hence his mercy to Adam Easton and his feeble resistance to the anti-papal legislation in England. At the same time Richard II was in trouble in England and could not afford to lose the support of the Pope, however hard pressed the Pope might be himself.

Cardinal Easton did not live to see the downfall

E

of his saviour, King Richard. He died in 1397 at Rome. He had been essentially a scholar before he became involved in the intrigues of the papal court. His works included a treatise on the election of a Pope, *De electione Pontificis*, a subject upon which, in view of his experience of the difficulties of Urban VI with an anti-pope, and his unpleasant experience of Urban's rule, he naturally had strong opinions. Other works were *De Potestate Ecclesiae* (no doubt arising from the disputes between the King and the Pope), *Defensorium Ecclesiae*, and a work on the form of procedure against heretics in which we may see an echo of his part against Wyclif. Earlier than these, whilst he was at Oxford, appeared his many works on Greek and Hebrew, now lost.

He is said to have written *Perfectio Vitae Spiritualis*, which sounds very much like a work for the use of contemplatives such as Walter Hilton's *Scala Perfectionis* and S. Edmund Rich's *Speculum*. Contemplatives flourished finely in England in the fourteenth century, and their writers, Rolle, Hilton, Julian of Norwich, and the anonymous author of *Denis Hid Divinity* and *Cloud of Unknowing*, have left us a heritage of profound spiritual literature unsurpassed in any age. It may astonish the moderns to find a man of affairs like Easton contributing to such

a group, but it would not have astonished the
fourteenth century. The relations between active and contemplative life were then better
understood.

CHAPTER III

THE KING'S MEN

I. PHILIP REPYNGDON

THE comparatively short reign of Henry IV saw three Englishmen in the Sacred College, Philip Repyngdon, Thomas Langley, and Robert Hallam, each of whom acted to considerable effect in both English and papal affairs. It may be part of the general distress of the Church, a consequence of the difficulties and decline of power of the Papacy during the years of schism when two and even three Popes struggled for supremacy, but it is significant that from this time onwards the English Cardinals cease to receive that unanimous commendation which was accorded to their predecessors. Their lives no longer follow the blameless paths of pious scholarship, wise statesmanship and just administration. They slip more readily into heresy, political intrigue and the follies of personal ambition. Most of them are still learned men and comparatively good men, but their lapses and indiscretions are more patent, a cause of scandal. Within the next century and a half there will be a few wicked, a few no better than they ought to be, and at least one saint.

The first of the English Cardinals in the fifteenth century was Philip Repyngdon. Though his origins are obscure we have ample light on his public life. He began very badly at Oxford by becoming an ardent and prominent supporter of John Wyclif, for which error he was condemned by the Synod of Blackfriars in 1382. Within a few months he forswore his heresies and was absolved. It is a testimony to his distinction and ability that it did not take him long to live down his lapse into Lollardy, for within twelve years he was Abbot of the Canons Regular of S. Augustine at the Abbey of S. Mary de Prè, Leicester, where, a century later, death cheated the King's gallows of Cardinal Wolsey.

We shall not have a very high opinion of Repyngdon if we judge him by his choice of friends. Wyclif was an injudicious choice ; Henry Bolingbroke, the usurper Henry IV, was a more judicious choice though not more admirable. But between the headstrong, turbulent and truculent Yorkshire reformer and John of Gaunt's traitorous son, who probably murdered the King his cousin and certainly murdered the Archbishop of York, there is not much to choose as a suitable friend for a Prince of the Church. John of Gaunt had supported the Lollards, not for principle but for policy, and his royal son was no less broad-minded.

When Philip Repyngdon became associated with him Henry was not yet king, nor had he any immediate prospect of achieving the crown. But when he did turn out Richard he chose Repyngdon, now Chancellor of the University of Oxford, as his royal chaplain and confessor.

In 1404 the royal chaplain was made Bishop of Lincoln by papal provision (the Statute of Provisors again notwithstanding), for Henry IV, like his predecessors and successors, only remembered the anti-papal statutes on suitable occasions. It was not long before the Statute of Provisors was found to have operated very much to the damage of the seats of learning by interfering with the papal choice of scholars and substituting the King's choice of favourites to receive the temporal rewards of the Church.

Repyngdon, though undoubtedly a learned man —his *Sermons on the Gospels* are still extant for us to judge—was also, as Antony à Wood, who had no special reason to flatter him, tells us, ' a powerful and God-fearing man, a lover of truth and hater of avarice.' Yet he clearly owed his eminence, possibly even his Red Hat, to Henry IV, for Pope Gregory XII, contending with his enemies, was not in a position to refuse what was in his power to grant to a strong king. He created

Philip Repyngdon Cardinal-priest of SS. Nereus and Achilleis on September 18, 1408, and allowed him, contrary to precedent, to retain his English bishopric. He nearly lost his Cardinalate by the deposition of Gregory XII, but as the Pope was restored in order to resign, the Cardinal was saved.

As Bishop of Lincoln he was active against the Lollards and granted a general licence to Oxford graduates to preach in his diocese. He resigned the bishopric in 1419 and died five years later. His request to lie in his old Abbey of S. Mary de Pré was not granted, but he was accorded the honour of burial beside his illustrious predecessor Grosseteste, at Lincoln.

II. THOMAS LANGLEY

When Archbishop Scrope of York had been murdered by order of Henry Bolingbroke for his association with the supporters of the Earl of March, the lawful heir to the throne of Richard II, the same Henry as King chose Thomas Langley to succeed the Archbishop. Langley, after leaving Cambridge, had joined the household of ' time-honoured Lancaster,' Henry's father. But Pope Innocent VII, disliking the murder of Archbishops, declined to approve the choice. Thomas Langley, said by some to have been a Yorkshireman, was already Dean of York and had succeeded Henry Beaufort, another future Cardinal, as Lord Chancellor. The Pope could not wisely ignore a man of such eminence and favour with the King. He could not decently allow the King to make Archbishops of York as fast as he murdered them. So he made Langley instead Prince-Bishop of the County Palatine of Durham, and named Robert Hallam, also a future Cardinal, for the Archbishopric of York.

But if the Pope would not have the King's man, the King would not have the Pope's, so Hallam resigned his benefices and went into the service of the papal court. He also was compensated with a Bishopric, Salisbury, two years later.

At Durham Langley ruled ably and magnificently, founding grammar and plain-song schools and building and repairing many churches.

He attended the General Council at Pisa as proctor for several English prelates, and was created Cardinal, without a title, by Pope John XXIII on June 6, 1411, along with Robert Hallam.

As a statesman in addition to serving twice as Lord Chancellor he was sent on embassies by Henry IV in 1409 and 1410 and by Henry V in 1414 to Paris to conclude the truce which preceded the Battle of Agincourt. He was actively concerned in the Treaty of Durham and in later negotiations with the Scots. He was Chancellor for the second time during the last five years of the reign of Henry V and the first two of Henry VI.

It was towards the end of the reign of Henry V that both Universities presented petitions against the Statute of Provisors, because the schools had suffered so severely from the lack of that encouragement which was formerly supplied by the papal preference for men of talents and industry who had graduated. The bishops, who exercised rights of presentation denied to the Pope, opposed the petition, and a compromise was effected whereby a proportion of benefices were ordered to be allocated to graduates of the Universities.

Henry VI succeeded his father in 1422 at the age of nine months. For the first two crucial years of his reign Cardinal Thomas Langley was Lord Chancellor of England, a more onerous and actively executive office then than it is to-day. The King's factious uncles, the Dukes of Gloucester and Bedford, did not make the office exactly easy, and the maintenance of order and the administration of justice needed all the ability and diplomacy of Langley. Soon after he ceased to be Chancellor, Joan the Maid arose in France and put an end to English domination there. From this time we have little record of Langley's public activities. He died in 1437, having been a Cardinal for twenty-six years, and was buried in the

Galilee Porch of his cathedral at Durham, where his tomb remains. He made munificent bequests to libraries at Cambridge and Oxford.

III. ROBERT HALLAM

Robert Hallam, having missed the Archbishopric of York and gone into the service of the Pope, was consecrated Bishop of Salisbury by Gregory XII at Siena in 1407. That the King, Henry IV, did not take this ill despite his Statutes of Provisors, is clear from the fact that at the Council of Pisa, which Hallam attended with Langley, he acted as ambassador from England with full powers to bind the English clergy to any decision which might be arrived at to heal the schism in the Papacy.

His career touches Langley's again when they are created Cardinals together by Pope John XXIII on June 6, 1411. Both creations were without title. It has been said that he did not receive a title in the customary manner because he never went to Rome for it, and this, coupled with the fact that when he attended the Council of Constance in 1414 he ranked as a Bishop and not a Cardinal, has cast some doubt on the authenticity of his Cardinalate, but there is ample contemporary evidence that he was a Cardinal. At

Constance he was the leading English representative amongst over a hundred English bishops, abbots and theologians, and he frequently appeared at this time as English spokesman.

It was declared at this Council, in support of the English claim to continue separate and equal representation in the Councils of the Church, that ' the Kingdom of England, thanks be to God, has never swerved from its obedience to the Roman Church ; it has never tried to rend the seamless coat of our Lord ; it has never tried to throw off its allegiance to the Roman Pontiffs.'

Cardinal Hallam gave England's assent to the suspension of John XXIII and was foremost in urging reform in the Papacy and Curia and in the Church in general. He assisted at the investigation into the charges against the pseudo-Pope Benedict XIII, he was also actively concerned in the prosecution of the heretics Huss and Jerome of Prague.

We have little personal record of this great Englishman. Before he became the Pope's nominee for the Archbishopric of York he had been successively Prebendary of Salisbury and York, Archdeacon of Canterbury and Chancellor of Oxford University. His universal fame may be judged by the tribute paid to him after his death at Gottlieben Castle, when he was buried with great pomp in the presence of the Emperor and all the Council at the foot of the steps leading to the high altar of Constance Cathedral. His motto says : ' I will sing the mercies of the Lord for ever.'

IV. Henry Beaufort

In Henry Beaufort we meet an altogether new type of Englishman in the Sacred College. Hitherto the English Cardinals have been men of the people, if we except the remote possibility of Thomas Langley's connection with Edmund de Langley, first Duke of York and son of Edward III. The eighteen of them of whom we have definite record were a very worthy lot of men, able and virtuous, good scholars, good priests and upright administrators. The captious might question Langton's secular activities against John, and, with more justice, Curzon's crusading operations against the Albigensians, Langham's wealth, Easton's intrigues which brought him to the dungeon of Nocera, Repyngdon's flirtations with Lollardy and friendship with Henry IV. But at the worst this leaves the eighteen with a very creditable record. Not even in these few cases has much wickedness been proved against any one of the Cardinals. Considering the number of Cardinals which popular opinion consigned to hell, the Englishmen, mostly of obscure and humble origin, acquitted themselves as well as any eighteen men in the Middle Ages, born in sin and bound in the frailty of the flesh, could be expected to do.

By the time Henry Beaufort, a royal Plantagenet, son of John of Gaunt, half-brother of Henry IV and uncle of Henry V, is raised to the purple, we are approaching that leap into the dark known as the Reformation. Wyclif has had his say, Huss and Jerome have strutted across the stage. Soon the zealots are going to give the Church, which needs reform, the very devil. The jealousy of princes, the frailties of prelates, the factions of popes, have put the Church in great distress. Before long the interference of temporal princes with the election of popes and prelates is going to fill the high places of the Church with even more worldly men, and her distress will be greater still.

In Henry Beaufort we have an excellent example of this new menace to the Church. It is not that Beaufort was an evil fellow, or even that he was not a good man as men go. He was certainly not a born bishop. The Church at this time needed Bishops.

It would be unfair to Henry Beaufort to ignore the handicaps with which he started life. In the first place he was the illegitimate son of John of Gaunt by his mistress Catherine Swynford. The mere illegitimacy was no great handicap ; it was removed by a special Act in 1397 after his parents

married, when he was already of age. It had
not prevented his obtaining prebendal stalls at
Lincoln (about the age of twelve and fourteen)
and the deanery of Wells at twenty. His next step,
at the age of twenty-one or thereabouts, was to be
elected Bishop of Lincoln, a year later Chancellor
of Oxford University, and four years later (now
twenty-six) Chancellor of England. In the next
year he succeeded the incomparable Wykeham,
who had died eighty years old, in the Bishopric of
Winchester.

These incidents in the career of the young man
were naturally not unconnected with the fact that
he was the grandson of Edward III and half-
brother of the King. They were some little compensation for being born the son of John of Gaunt.
That handicap itself was not so easy to live down.
His forbears—Edward III was the best of them
—had not been the most amiable of men. His
father, though he has been eulogized by Shakespeare, was thoroughly hated by his contemporaries, who knew better. The common people
who, before the days of an inspired press, could
be relied upon to form a pretty just estimate of
those under whom they suffered, set fire to Gaunt's
palace of Savoy and reversed his arms as a traitor's.
They knew what sort of influence he had exerted
during the decline of Edward III and the minority
of Richard II. He had supported the hot-headed

Wyclif, opposed the great and good Wykeham. He had fostered his son's usurpation of the throne, and his son was popularly believed to have connived at or inspired the death of Richard. He was hardly the kindest and the best of men, the sort of father a future Cardinal would choose. It is possible that Beaufort felt a genuine vocation for the clerical life, but if he did it was rather a pity to spoil it by making him a pluralist prodigy. We need not blame him for his early advancement in the Church. We may marvel that in spite of it he achieved many things and died a tolerably good man, Shakespeare notwithstanding.

Beaufort was Chancellor again when Henry V came to the throne in 1413, and as Henry's uncle was his friend, guide and counsellor. The confidence which Henry gave him should be sufficient answer to those who charged him with offences against the King, and it was brought forward as such when Beaufort was later accused on this score by the Duke of Gloucester, Henry's brother. The Bishop was sent on an embassy to France in 1414, attending the Council of Constance, with Hallam and Langley, in the royal rather than the national interest, and achieved diplomatic success with the Emperor Sigismund on Henry's behalf. The new Pope, elected through this Council as a solution to the problem of three conflicting popes, was Martin V. He owed a good deal to the influence of the English Crown, probably not a little to Beaufort personally, so he proposed to create him Cardinal and legate to England. This raised an unexpected difficulty. Chicheley, Archbishop of Canterbury and Primate, could see a grave danger to his authority in the continuous presence in England of a legate who would not only be senior to him in ecclesiastical rank, but have the added advantage of royal blood and secular pre-eminence. The King, moved by this, and possibly pressure from Gloucester his brother, forbade Beaufort to accept the dignity. There the matter rested for a while. The Bishop made a pilgrimage to Jerusalem.

Before Henry V died, he had named Beaufort guardian of his nine-months'-old son, Henry VI. The peers spiritual and temporal forming the Council, with very great care and respect for the forms of procedure, appointed Humphrey, Duke of Gloucester, president of the Council and protector, his brother of Bedford becoming regent in France. The Council always took the greatest precaution to prevent any trespass on the sovereign authority by Gloucester, and in this it was wise. It is impossible not to suspect the influence of Beaufort in this care for the rights of Parliament and the young King, and in the limitation of Gloucester's authority and power. It was inevitable that a man of Beaufort's capacity should overrule his nephews Bedford and Gloucester. It was equally inevitable that Gloucester should resent his uncle's power and influence. Gloucester was able, vigorous and ambitious. He is known as Good Duke Humphrey. He was only relatively good, not in the sense that Albert, Consort of Queen Victoria, was good. He was good to men of letters, seats of learning and the Abbey of S. Albans. Naturally the chroniclers would not call that bad. But so far as Beaufort was concerned, Gloucester was for ruling England, carrying war into France against the Dauphin whom Joan made King, and taking to wife Jacqueline of Bavaria, heiress of Hainault, Holland, Zealand and Friesland, a tempting prize. As a man of peace, the Bishop, possibly jealous of his nephew's power, opposed all these projects, but only the first successfully. From this arose a permanent enmity between Beaufort and Gloucester.

In 1424 Beaufort was again Chancellor and virtually ruled the country. He was very rich. It was questioned (by Gloucester) whether he could become so rich honestly. He had lent both the late King and the present King very large sums of money, and so added the vast power of the money-lender to that of the royal uncle, prelate and Chancellor. His strong opposition to Good Duke Humphrey's attempt to snatch the inheritance of Jacqueline from under the angry noses

F

of various European claimants, brought about open conflict between them. The dispute was settled temporarily by the return of Bedford.

Beaufort resigned the Chancellorship and returned with Bedford to Calais, where he received the title of Cardinal-priest of S. Eusebius from Pope Martin V. This was in 1426 when he was about fifty. He received the Red Hat at Mechlin and was appointed *legate a latere* in Germany, Hungary and Bohemia, and captain-general of the crusade against the Hussites of Bohemia. This was work more after the heart of the grandson of the greatest knight in Europe and prelate of his grandfather's famous Order of the Garter, the greatest Order of medieval chivalry. Peace was all very well when Good Duke Humphrey wanted to ravage France and start a dog fight by coveting the lands of an heiress of easy virtue. But there is war and war, and hammering the Hussites is the war for a fighting Bishop, Cardinal and papal legate. He fought as valiantly as any other crusader, and it is related that when the Germans fled a second time after he had rallied them, he tore down the standard of the Empire and flung it after them.

Meanwhile Duke Humphrey at home is once more put kindly and firmly in his place by Parliament. For the Cardinal-crusader to return to England in full pomp at this time may have been a little too much for the Duke or the Council, and Parliament may have been alarmed on its own account at the return of the great man yet more great. He was welcomed with honour but treated with suspicion, and required to promise to do nothing in his ecclesiastical capacity derogatory to the rights of King and Kingdom. He was too old a statesman to demur. Within a very short time he was invited to take his place on the Council and loaded with solemn flattery by Parliament.

To achieve this he adopted the simple means of accepting a bribe and breaking his trust. There is something in the political atmosphere which has an ill effect upon the best of men. Beaufort was not a bad man. Yet he was not quite the best of men. He was far better when at Winchester than he was at Westminster. Bribery has been common enough at Westminster throughout its history. Nevertheless it ill becomes a Bishop of Winchester, Cardinal and rich great-uncle of the King. Even the fact that it was highly appreciated by Parliament and the people does not make it excusable.

The circumstances, briefly, were these. The Cardinal, as Captain-General of the anti-Hussite Crusade, was given royal licence to publish the crusade and raise an expedition of two hundred and fifty lancers and twenty-five hundred archers, on the reasonable condition that they should be armed and provisioned within the realm. For a bribe of one thousand marks the Captain-General led his men when he crossed to the continent, not against the Hussites, but against Charles VII and the King's enemies in France. His incredible excuse, unworthy of so able and experienced a statesman, was that he dared not disobey the orders of his sovereign and the men refused to march against the Hussites until they had restored the glory of English arms in France. The excuse deceived no one, but his disgraceful behaviour restored him to the favour of Parliament.

In the next scene he wears the pontificals at Notre Dame and crowns Henry VI, King of England, King of France, six months after Bedford had burned Joan the Maid at Rouen.

In his absence on this occasion Good Duke Humphrey obtained against the Cardinal a writ of praemunire, a weapon like its fellow the Statute of Provisors ever handy to the spiteful against prosperous prelates. Beaufort, now recovering his good sense, found it convenient to be called to Rome whilst the King returned to England. Soon after the King's return a bill of indemnity against the penalties of praemunire, if incurred, was passed in favour of the Cardinal, and he returned in breathless haste to defend his reputation. It was, despite the indemnity, a courageous thing to do, though the time was chosen with discretion. He challenged his accusers to come forward, but none came, and he cautiously obtained a formal declaration of his innocence over the King's signature. That was another round won against Good Duke Humphrey. He fought one more. This concerned the liberation of the Duke of Orleans, a prisoner in England, to work for peace in France. The Cardinal favoured it; the Duke opposed it, and lost.

The conference at Arras in 1433, the most representative meeting of the kind Europe had yet seen, was brought about by Beaufort in his efforts to secure peace in France and Europe generally. It failed. The Cardinal continued to oppose war with France, but when his opposition proved definitely ineffective he did the right thing. He lent vigorous support, especially financial, to bring the war to a victorious end for his own country. His financial ability was of great value to the nation in any crisis, and it was no doubt responsible for much of his power. Yet, though he had use of sums far greater than he could have earned in his civil or ecclesiastical capacities, he maintained a sound reputation for integrity. Whatever may have been alleged against him by his enemies in this connection, nothing was ever proved. As financier he retained the confidence of all classes to the end.

His later years were spent, properly enough, in

his diocese, where he completed the work on Winchester Cathedral and the Almshouse of the Holy Cross left unfinished by Wykeham. Both these buildings remain, monuments to his munificence.

He died, about seventy years old, in 1447, not in agony and despair, but in the peace and comfort of the consolations of his religion. His riches were disposed in charity. Shakespeare's picture of Beaufort's death in *Henry VI* has as much relation to fact as the picture of Bottom asking for a bottle of hay. There is no reason why the dramatic devices of the playwright should be mistaken for, or preferred to, the facts of contemporary record and the judgment of the historian. Shakespeare was not an historian.

V. John Kempe

Amongst the accusations made by Good Duke Humphrey against Cardinal Beaufort was that he had contrived to arrogate all the powers of government to himself and his creature the Archbishop of York. This 'creature' was John Kempe, son of a gentleman of Kent and the greatest ecclesiastical lawyer of his day. He must have been invaluable on this account to Beaufort, and the Cardinal may be congratulated on the wisdom with which he chose his man. Kempe gave Beaufort constant and loyal service, and he was therefore always opposed to Humphrey, Duke of Gloucester ; and evidently the Duke felt this opposition keenly.

When the infant Henry VI succeeded to the crown, Kempe was a member of the Council. Born about 1380, he had been educated at Merton College, Oxford, where he was Fellow, and had a brilliant career in law. By 1415 he was Dean of the Court of Arches and Vicar-General to the Archbishop of Canterbury. He was successively Archdeacon of Durham, Keeper of the Privy Seal, Bishop of Rochester, Chichester (where he never officiated) and London. During these years he had been frequently employed on embassies by Henry V. At the time of that monarch's death he was Chancellor of Normandy.

When Beaufort became Cardinal in 1426, his creature became Archbishop of York and Chancellor of England, holding that office until Gloucester gained power in 1432. He was unpopular at York because he was put there against the wishes of the Crown and Chapter, but he would have been unpopular in any case because he was a most unsatisfactory bishop anywhere. He was a bishop only because the legal profession was not yet organized to secure adequate rewards for its experts. English law was still in process of complication, lawyers were as yet ravelling it for future lawyers to unravel more profitably. Church bene-

fices were the readiest means of rewarding such a
man as Kempe. He was a man of sound morals,
wise and upright. But he was no bishop. He
was an example of one of the many abuses of
ecclesiastical office which ultimately reduced the
Church to that pass which made the revolt in
England possible. He was not to blame. Nevertheless his successive dioceses suffered severely by
his enforced neglect and his incapacity for episcopal duty. He was a lawyer and diplomat, and
the Church as well as the State needed such.

On behalf of Beaufort he led the English embassy to the conference at Arras, which failed
because the English demands, stiffened by
Gloucester, were excessive. A few years later,
in 1439, he was created Cardinal-priest of S.
Balbina by Pope Eugenius IV.

As in the case of Beaufort's elevation, Chicheley
Archbishop of Canterbury was rightly nervous
about possible intrusion on his authority by Cardinals resident in England, and he was naturally
enough especially apprehensive when the new Cardinal was Archbishop of York, and so rival for
the Primacy. His position was certainly difficult.
It was not made easier by his support of Gloucester, though that support was more actually opposition to Beaufort. Still, he could evidently take
care of himself and his See, for he held it for thirty
years.

After the deaths of Gloucester and Beaufort, Kempe continued to maintain the Lancastrian cause against de la Pole, Duke of Suffolk, and the Yorkists, and in 1450 after the death of Suffolk he became Lord Chancellor. It was largely owing to his diplomatic tactics that the rebellion in this year of the men of Kent under Jack Cade was broken. He was in his element on such an occasion.

In 1452 Kempe was translated by papal provision (Statute of Provisors once more notwithstanding) from York to Canterbury, and it is evidence of the esteem in which he was held by the Pope that Nicholas V created a new Cardinal-Bishopric for him by splitting that of Porto and S. Rufina, and conferring the latter title upon him. He showed considerable bravery when threatened by the Yorkists, who were gaining strength rapidly in his last years. He died at Lambeth in 1454. The only memorial of his episcopal office which he left was a college of secular priests and a fine new church for his native place, Wye.

VI. THOMAS BOURCHIER

We have yet another example of the new type of prelate under which the Church in England suffered in Thomas Bourchier. He was the second

English Cardinal of royal blood, a great-grandson of Edward III through his mother Lady Anne Plantagenet, cousin of Cardinal Beaufort. It is not denied that he was a very able man, a sound statesman, a man of peace, personally popular, a patron of the arts and therefore, on the whole, a good man. But he was not good for the Church. He was too much of a statesman to attend to his episcopal duties, and the resulting neglect gave free play to every sort of delinquency and abuse in the flocks under his care.

It is not surprising that after a few Primates like Kempe and Bourchier and bishops like Beaufort, the reformers should find ample excuse for their attacks on the Church. It was not a matter of an odd misfit bishop here and there. It was a succession of misfits in the principal sees and especially in the Primacy. Bourchier, like Kempe, was Archbishop of Canterbury. With the central authority in the Church at first weak through internal dissension and then weak through the intrusion of personal villainy by the domination of temporal powers, the Church in England needed bishops who were orthodox and strong disciplinarians. She got lawyers, statesmen and royal uncles who were too busy elsewhere to care for much more than receiving the fruits of their benefices. It is true that the Church was the only place for lawyers and diplomats, and the Church needed them as much then as she does to-day. But now it is not necessary to make them bishops to give them adequate reward and dignity. Whether or not it was necessary in the fifteenth century it was the practice. Hence, partly, the turmoil of the sixteenth century.

Bourchier's progress, like Beaufort's, was a typical instance of the abuse of Church patronage. He collected benefices far and wide at an early age, or rather they were heaped upon him. He held several livings before he was ordained acolyte and sub-deacon. In 1424, being aged about eighteen, he was Prebendary of Lichfield, in 1434 Chancellor of Oxford University and Bishop of Worcester. He was chosen Bishop of Ely by the Chapter, either because that was a politic thing to do or because they thought he would make an ideal bishop, but King Henry VI, or his advisers, declined to hand over the temporalities. So the See was administered by Louis of Luxembourg, Cardinal and Archbishop of Rouen, on whose death Bourchier obtained possession. In February 1454-5 he was translated to Canterbury, succeeding Cardinal Kempe, and soon after became Lord Chancellor of England.

It is now that he begins to play an operative part in English history. The birth of an heir to Henry VI had deprived the Duke of York of his chance of succession. The King's temporary

insanity had enabled York to assume power as Protector, but his recovery put an end even to
that, and the Wars of the Roses began in earnest.
Bourchier was naturally, by birth, a Lancastrian,
but he used his influence in support of Henry for
peace rather than in opposing York. When the
Earl of Warwick placed Edward Duke of York
on the throne as Edward IV, deposing Henry,
Archbishop Bourchier crowned him King in 1461
and married him to Elizabeth Woodville in 1465.
When the court became infested with Woodvilles
and Greys, the tide so far turned against Edward that he was made prisoner by Warwick, the
man who had made him King. The Archbishop
was logically and justly on Edward's side, supporting, as he should, the King accepted by the
nation through Parliament. Warwick, when the
King was free again, went to London, released
Henry VI and made him King once more. Bourchier, though nominally and formally acquiescent,
remained loyal to Edward IV and saw him eventually victorious and secure, Henry being then
dead. On account of all this he has been accused
of being double, since on one morning he conducted Henry, in his royal robes, through the city,
and in the afternoon gave orders for the admittance
of Edward through a postern in the walls. His
conduct may as justly be called non-partisan or impartial, as double. It was such, at least, that neither

side took steps to blame him for it, and he remained to act as mediator.

This was in 1471. A few years earlier the Archbishop had been named Cardinal by Pope Paul II on Friday, September 18, 1467, though it was six years later before he received the Red Hat with the title of Cardinal-priest of S. Cyriacus in Thermis.

On the death of Edward IV in 1483, the Cardinal, when Richard Duke of Gloucester was in possession of the capital and practically of the kingdom, pledged himself to Edward's widow for the good conduct of the Duke, and prevailed upon her to allow her son Richard to leave the sanctuary at Westminster and join his brother, the young King, in the Tower. There they were both murdered. Doubt has been cast upon the version of Bourchier's part in this affair, supplied by Sir Thomas More, who may have had it from eye-witnesses, but whatever the details of the matter, Bourchier's pledge was worthless whether he knew it or not, and it is no credit to his intelligence if he did not know it. In this matter he was either a knave or a fool. Richard had only just come from murdering Hastings and imprisoning the Archbishop of York and the Bishop of Ely, Morton, a future Cardinal and successor to Bourchier

Whether or not Bourchier played double here again with the Queen-mother, his actions would have made little difference. Gloucester was supreme and was determined literally to kill opposition.   Within a few weeks the Cardinal-Primate crowned the usurper Gloucester, Richard III. Within two years more Richard was dead, and the aged Cardinal crowned his last King, Henry VII, Earl of Richmond, a Beaufort and Lancastrian.   In January 1485-6 he formally healed the breach between York and Lancaster by marrying Henry VII to Elizabeth of York.   He died the following year at Knowle, eighty years old.

It must have required no small skill on Bourchier's part to live unharmed in body or fame through those turbulent times and to hold the Primacy unscathed for thirty years.   It should not rashly be assumed that his office accounted entirely for his immunity ; civil strife had not long before cost a predecessor, Sudbury, and Scrope Archbishop of York their lives.   He is credited with having worked consistently to make peace during the Wars of the Roses, and he was one of the four arbitrators at the Peace of Amiens in 1475.

His hospitality was lavish, in keeping with the customs of his time, and he is known to have entertained Hambois and Taverner the musicians, Tiptoft Earl of Worcester the scholar, Botoner, chronicler and traveller, and an Eastern Patriarch, probably Peter II of Antioch.   He certainly kept his state as a Prince of the Church, though the Church in his care languished in consequence.

VII. John Morton

In Sir Thomas More's *Utopia* you may read of
' that reverend prelate John Morton, Archbishop
of Canterbury, Cardinal, and Chancellor of England ; a man (for Mr. More knows well what he
was) that was not less venerable for his wisdom
and virtues, than for the high character that he
bore ; he was of a middle stature, not broken with
age ; his looks begot reverence rather than fear ;
his conversation was easy, but serious and grave ;
he took pleasure sometimes to try the force of
those that came as suitors to him upon business,
by speaking sharply, though decently to them, and
by that he discovered their spirit and presence of
mind ; with which he was much delighted, when
it did not grow up to an impudence, as bearing a
great resemblance to his own temper ; and he
looked on such persons as the fittest men for
affairs. He spoke both gracefully and weightily ;
he was eminently skilled in the law, and had a vast
understanding and a prodigious memory ; and
those excellent talents with which nature had fur-
nished him were improved by study and experience. When I was in England, the King depended
much on his counsel, and the Government seemed
to be chiefly supported by him ; for from his
youth up, he had been all along practised in affairs ;

and having passed through many traverses of fortune, he had acquired to his great cost a vast stock of wisdom ; which is not soon lost, when it is purchased so dear.'

Mr. More, who wrote this account of Cardinal John Morton, ' knew well what he was,' because he had been a page in the Cardinal's household. More himself was later Lord Chancellor. He possessed one of the keenest minds of his day. He was as honest an English gentleman as ever lived. Therefore we need no better account of the character of this great Cardinal.

Morton was born at Milbourne S. Andrews, Dorset, in 1420, educated by the Benedictines of Cerne Abbey, graduated B.C.L. at Balliol College, became Principal of Peckwater Inn, Oxford, and practised in the Court of Arches, thus following the profession of his patron Cardinal Bourchier. He could not have followed a safer man in his day. It was natural that he should obtain considerable preferment ; he was, among other things, sub-dean of Lincoln and prebendary of Salisbury and Lincoln.

His early association with Cardinal Bourchier would explain his being a Lancastrian, even if he had no other reason. But he did not succeed in holding the middle course so successfully as Bourchier—he was younger, more vigorous-minded and possibly more honest. ' Dr. Morton, parson of

Blokesworth, who,' as Lingard relates, 'had been present in the field at Towton,' had been in consequence attainted by the Yorkists and had fled with the redoubtable Margaret of Anjou.

After Tewkesbury, ten years later, he petitioned King Edward IV that he was ' as sorrowful and repentant as any creature may be,' and so secured the reversal of the attainder. So far he had not achieved high office, but his abilities had obviously made him recognized as a man to be reckoned with. From this time his progress was rapid. He had already become Master of the Rolls ; he now gained the Archdeaconry of Winchester and then that of Chester. In 1474 he went on an embassy to Hungary, and in the following year assisted Bourchier in the negotiation of the treaty of Pec-quigny. In 1478 he was elected Bishop of Ely, and we have a fine picture of the temper of the man in his walking barefooted and fasting from his residence at Downham to Ely to be installed and afterwards say his Mass.

On the death of Edward IV, which he witnessed, Morton found himself once more on the wrong side. His loyalty to Edward and Edward's children, young Edward V and his brother Richard Duke of York, put him badly out of favour with Richard Crookback Duke of Gloucester, and it would appear that that unlovely murderer found the Bishop of Ely a more difficult problem than the Cardinal-Archbishop Bourchier.

When Richard was removing the several obstacles between himself and the throne, he prevailed upon Bourchier, as we have seen already, to let the young Duke of York join his brother in the Tower so that they could both be smothered together. He adopted a different method with Morton. When he visited the council chamber in the Tower and wanted the Bishop out of the way in order to murder Lord Hastings, the story, according to Shakespeare, runs prettily enough thus :

Gloucester : ' My lord of Ely ! '

Ely : ' My lord ? '

Gloucester : ' When I was last in Holborn I saw good strawberries in your garden there. I do beseech you send for some of them.'

Ely : ' Marry and will, my lord, with all my heart.'

Whereupon the Bishop sent his servant away for the strawberries, and the Duke clapped the Bishop and the Archbishop of York into prison ; and Hastings was led from the council chamber to a log on the green at the door of the chapel, where his head was struck off.

The prison and the murder part of this affair are historic facts enough, whether or not the strawberries came into the business. It is more than likely that the Bishop did grow fine strawberries in the garden of his palace in Ely Place, adjoining his chapel of S. Etheldreda, which has in recent years been restored to its ancient faith and use. And as the time was the third week in June, they should have been ripe enough.

Gloucester now being King, Ely remained under lock and key, first in the Tower, then at Brecknock Castle, whence he escaped abroad, by way of Ely, until Richard received the first instalment of his deserts at Bosworth. The new King, Henry VII, was far too astute to lose the services of John Morton. The Bishop was called home and made Privy Councillor and Chancellor of the Duchy of Cornwall. He was translated to the Archbishopric of Canterbury to succeed Bourchier in 1486, became Lord Chancellor in the following year, and wielded such influence with the King and Government as More has observed. More entered his service in 1491.

It has been alleged with some reason that the *Life of Richard III* formerly attributed to More was Morton's, translated by More. Which fact may partly account for the true character given to the King. Either way, it is clear that More concurs.

Morton was created Cardinal-priest of S. Anastasia by Pope Alexander VI in 1493, being now an old man. Two years later he received the Chancellorship of Oxford University. He died, renowned and respected, in 1500, having achieved, like his patron and predecessor, the full round age of fourscore. He was primarily, like Beaufort, Kempe and Bourchier, a statesman and lawyer, but he was also a better Bishop than either. Morton's Dyke is evidence of his drainage of the Fens.

VIII. CHRISTOPHER BAINBRIDGE

With Cardinal Christopher Bainbridge we approach the beginning of the end of Catholic England. He is typical of his immediate predecessors in being less of a priest than a man of affairs, and as in Morton we have seen this type at its best, in Bainbridge we see it somewhere near its worst. He arose just as the effect of unpriestly clerics was culminating in the Church. In England the Church had reached the state which was to be expected when the principle whereby men like Beaufort, Kempe, Bourchier, Morton and Bainbridge achieved high office in Church and State had permeated her organization. The worst effects of spiritual neglect were being felt. The Popes, instead of seizing upon the prosperity and comparative peace of the times to repair the damage done in the period of the Papacy's trial, were seeking to extend their earthly dominions in the manner of temporal princes. Christopher Bain-

bridge, lawyer and soldier, was just the man for
that.

He was born about 1464 at Hilton, Westmor-
land, and read law at Oxford. His public life did
not start, so far as we know, quite so early as usual
for such men in those days. But at thirty-one he
was Provost of Queen's College, and soon after,
in fairly rapid succession, he was Prebendary of
Salisbury and Lincoln, Treasurer of the Diocese
of London, Archdeacon of Surrey, Dean of York,
Dean of Windsor, Master of the Rolls, and in 1507
Bishop of Durham on the nomination of Henry
VII. In 1508 he was translated by the Pope to
the Archbishopric of York.

On the accession of Henry VIII, Archbishop
Bainbridge went to Rome as the young King's
ambassador to Pope Julius II, and two years later,
in 1511, was created by that Pontiff Cardinal-
priest of S. Praxedes for negotiating the support
of Henry for the Pope against France. He was
now in the thick of European politics, a sphere
which England had newly entered, and in which
the next Cardinal, Thomas Wolsey, was to distinguish himself above all others.

Since the King of France, by waging war against
the Pope, had forfeited his title of ' Most Christian
King,' Bainbridge endeavoured to obtain it for
his master Henry, who appears to have had a particular fondness for papal titles of the kind,

' Defender of the Faith ' being his favourite, which he bequeathed to his successors. In this business Bainbridge failed because the King of France made peace.

The new Cardinal, though originally and still nominally the King's man, was now the Pope's man too. As the legate and general, he led the papal army to the siege and capture of Ferrara. So far as England was concerned he was always a zealous agent in the King's interest at Rome and a vigorous enemy of France.

There is not much doubt that he was a man of violent temper and no small arrogance, hence the story that he was poisoned by an Italian priest in his service, Rimaldo de Modena, is generally accepted.

He died thus, at the age of fifty, in 1514, and was buried in the Church of S. Thomas of Canterbury attached to the English Hospice, later the English College, Rome ; so he made way, both at York and in the Sacred College, for Thomas Wolsey.

IX. THOMAS WOLSEY

The most notorious Cardinal in English history appeared on the scene at the beginning of the critical period for the Church in England. His fame is not so closely connected with England's official repudiation of Rome as is popularly supposed, for he was dead before Henry VIII rejected the authority of the Pope. Nor is it due in any great extent to the affair of Henry's first divorce. Before this was broached Wolsey was probably the most powerful figure in Europe. Though the circumstances and the time were propitious, he owed no more to them than he did to his own exertions and ability. His career is that of a man who would have been foremost and famous in any age.

He was born at Ipswich of middle-class parents, that is, they were not titled nor were they in the lowest class. His father was a burgess of considerable possessions. The Church still offered the best opportunities for advancement and profit to the children of that class.

The Wolseys came a generation too soon for the distribution of Church loot which was to form the basis of big business careers. Thomas was born about 1471–4, a little later than Cardinal John Fisher, whose parents were in similar circumstances. But whereas Fisher went to Cambridge and pursued a scholastic and sacerdotal career, Wolsey used the Church, as did the half-dozen English Cardinals who preceded him, and indeed the majority who took orders at that time, for a stepping-stone to secular advancement. In this he did no more than share in that misuse of the highest ecclesiastical offices which had become a well-established practice. But his share was certainly the lion's share. It is doubtful whether he has ever been equalled as a pluralist. At one time or another he held very nearly every preferment of high value in England, many of them at the same time. He had not a vestige of the excuse that might have been fairly urged on behalf of the earlier pluralists. His pluralism was the amassing of personal wealth and distinction and no more. He raised the practice to a fine art and became its greatest master. Nor did he depend upon the assistance and favouritism of Henry VIII. He had achieved a considerable collection of benefices before that young monarch was in a position to help him.

Educated at Magdalen College, Oxford, and ordained priest in 1498, Wolsey had held several offices and benefices, including the rich Deanery of Lincoln, domestic chaplaincy to the Archbishop of Canterbury (Henry Deane), and finally was chaplain to Henry VII before that King died. Whatever he needed to learn about money-making, he could not have been in a better school than that in which Henry VII and his carrion Empson and Dudley were masters. Under the Archbishop of Canterbury and Sir Richard Nanfant (deputy of Calais), whose chaplain he was, and then under Henry VII when he was actively negotiating

THOMAS CARDINAL WOLSEY

foreign alliances and marriages, Wolsey gained his experience in diplomacy. For his earlier training in that art he could not have had a better master than Richard Foxe, Bishop of Winchester.

When Henry VIII became King at eighteen, Wolsey, though nearly twenty years his senior, was still a young man. He was well established at court, a man of affairs, with an attractive personality and an unrivalled capacity for making the most of his opportunities. Moreover, he was well off and lavish in display and entertainment, completely at home in the atmosphere of the court, not too much of the priest to disdain court extravagances or court vices. In short, he was the perfect favourite for a luxurious, personable and active young King who had inherited prosperity and prestige as the fruits of the cunning and avarice of his father. Henry became King at a more favourable time than any of his predecessors, a time of peace in England and Europe, and consequent increasing prosperity. Wolsey became almoner to Henry soon after his accession. The two were intimate friends. We need not be surprised, considering Wolsey's superior age, experience and ability, that he exerted great influence over the King. So far as the government of the nation was concerned, Jack was as good as, if not better than, his royal master. No prelate before or

since has held such sway in England. Nor has any
prelate used his power in the State more wisely.
It is a fact usually forgotten in the modern amaze-
ment at his power and extravagance, the modern
pecksniffian horror at his vices, that he used his
power with singular skill and ability to the advantage of his country as well as himself; that
although he was a proud prelate, luxurious and
ambitious, he was also a good deal more. We find
him, even in the early years of the young King's
extravagance, supporting his former patron the
Bishop of Winchester in a protest against the
ready way in which the Lord Treasurer provided
the money to burn.

Wolsey's position with the King became such
that he was the regular channel of approach to
the royal person, for both Englishmen and the
representatives of foreign princes. Consequently
his riches increased rapidly. As Henry grew he
took more power, yet his favourite advanced with
him. He was successively Dean of Hereford,
York, S. Stephen's Westminster, and Bishop of
Lincoln in the course of 1512-13. In the following
year he succeeded Cardinal Christopher Bainbridge as Archbishop of York.

By this time the King of England and his man
were in a singularly powerful position in Europe.
Their support was sought eagerly by the Emperor,
the Pope, and the King of France. Never had

England been in a position to interfere so effectively in the politics of Europe.

Henry had made war against France early in his reign, backed by Wolsey, but had in the first campaign failed. Later, in alliance with the Emperor Maximilian, he was more successful. In both cases he had served the useful purpose of obstructing the operations of the King of France against the Italian States and the Pope. Wolsey accompanied Henry in all his expeditions.

When Francis I succeeded Louis XII and Charles V succeeded Maximilian, Henry held the trump cards of the political game in Europe. Wolsey worked with subtle diplomacy, usually for peace, but always for strengthening the position of Henry, and therefore of Wolsey.

The Pope, Leo X, who was menaced by Francis I, needed the support of Henry. He created Wolsey Cardinal-priest of S. Cecilia trans Tiberim in 1515 and, later, papal legate. Archbishop Warham of Canterbury, anticipating the difficulty which his predecessors had suffered in such a position, made way for Wolsey in the Chancellorship, and the latter, after some hesitation, real or feigned, accepted the office.

It was not long before there was a clear prospect of Henry's becoming Emperor—he had been offered the succession by Maximilian—and Wolsey's becoming Pope. When Maximilian died

Henry sent his envoy to nominate him candidate for the Imperial crown if the electors could be made favourable, but the envoy, from lack of tact or funds, failed. Charles of Spain was chosen. Henry's election would have greatly increased Wolsey's chances at Rome—but he would have lost (as he did in any case) the block of fourteen votes on the conclave promised by Francis I in return for supporting his election in place of Charles. Francis was undoubtedly deceived by Henry and Wolsey.

Nevertheless, such was the English King's position, that before long Henry was invited to arbitrate between Charles and Francis. He sent Wolsey to act as his representative. The end of this affair was an alliance with the Pope and Charles V against Francis (the strong power) in pursuance of Wolsey's usual policy, a proceeding which was long premeditated and reflects no credit on the Cardinal's impartiality. Nevertheless he worked so skilfully, and his position was so strong, that Francis did not for a long time blame him (if indeed he fully realized the trick had been played on him), but continued to endeavour to gain the support of the English King.

On the death of Pope Leo X, both Henry and the Emperor supported Wolsey's candidature, but the Papacy was still independent enough of them, though malleable to other forces, for a Dutchman to be elected instead. When he, Adrian VI, died two years later, Wolsey made another bid, but was foiled by the strength of the French Cardinals in the conclave, and Giulio de Medici, who had baulked him on the previous occasion by giving his support to Adrian, was now elected Clement VII.

In the subsequent events on the continent, including the taking of Francis I by Charles at Pavia, his captivity, Henry's break with Charles, the release of Francis, and Henry's alliance with him, we see the Cardinal manipulating the situation, always to the advantage of England, Henry and Wolsey.

Yet despite Wolsey's commanding advantage in Europe, maintained by his consummate ability fired solely by ambition, he failed signally to gain his greatest objectives, either because, big as he was, he thought he was even bigger, or because he was never fully enough informed of the strength against him.

We may gain some rough idea of Wolsey's wealth by this time from the brief summary of his sources of income given by Lingard. ' As chancellor and legate he derived considerable emoluments from the courts over which he presided. He was also Archbishop of York ; he farmed the revenues of Hereford and Worcester . . . he held *in commendam* the abbey of S. Albans with the bishopric of Bath ; and afterwards, as the vacancies occurred, he exchanged Bath for the rich bishopric of Durham, and Durham for the administration of the still richer see of Winchester. To these sources of wealth should be added the presents and pensions which he received from foreign princes. Francis settled on him an annuity of twelve thousand livres, as a compensation for the bishopric of Tournai, and Charles V and Leo X granted him a yearly pension of seven thousand five hundred ducats from the revenues of the bishoprics of Toledo and Palencia in Spain.'

But Wolsey though greedy was not miserly. He spent as freely as he gained his wealth. He was a generous patron of literature, a typical Renaissance benefactor to seats of learning. He founded the college of Christ Church at Oxford, by papal authority, converting the monastery of S. Frideswide for the purpose. He maintained a sumptuous state and a vast retinue. It numbered over five hundred and included members of practically every important family in the land. His building of Hampton Court, which he gave to the King, his generous patronage of the arts and the delicate, cultured combination of strawberries and cream attributed to him by legend, mark him as a Renaissance figure with the authentic Medicean manner.

When the doctrines of Luther first found their

way into England, the Cardinal and the King actively opposed them. Henry's *Defence of the Seven Sacraments*, which obtained for him the title of ' Defender of the Faith,' so proudly passed on to his heretical successors, was popularly believed to have been supervised, at least, by Wolsey and Bishop Fisher of Rochester, the future Cardinal and martyr. Luther's subsequent abuse of the King and the Cardinal, *illud monstrum et publicum odium Dei et hominum, pestis illa regni tui*—abuse which from its source becomes almost a compliment —provoked Henry to an avowal of the work and a fine eulogy of his minister, ' whom he always loved, but whom he shall now love much more.'

In 1525 the matter of Henry's divorce from Catherine of Aragon was broached to Wolsey. There is little foundation for the popular belief that it was suggested to the King by Wolsey, except the fact that Wolsey appears to have approved of the project as suitable to his policy of strengthening the alliance between England and France by the marriage of Henry to Rénée, daughter of Louis XII. But there is no reason at all to suppose that Wolsey knew of the King's intentions with regard to Anne Boleyn, or if he did, that he expected those intentions to be carried out. Nor would he, by supporting the King, necessarily be conniving at divorce, the King's case being that the marriage had never been valid. When Henry disclosed his determination with regard to Anne Boleyn, the Cardinal, after objection and protest, agreed to support the King as usual. But it was not long before his conscience began to worry him in the matter, and he told the King that though he was, in gratitude, ready ' to spend his goods, blood and life ' in the service of his master, yet he was under greater obligations to God, to whom he would have to give account of his judgments. From this time until the arrival of Cardinal Campeggio as legate to deal with the affair jointly with Wolsey, the latter seems to have wavered, fearing to risk the fury of the King, yet uneasy in his conscience when he supported him. Campeggio's procedure and caution exhausted the King's patience. For this and the subsequent protraction, adjournments, and the withdrawal of the case to Rome, the King blamed Wolsey. The Cardinal's enemies seized their opportunities. He found himself in disgrace, lost his Chancellorship, and one after another his richest offices, until he was finally relegated to his see of York.

Here again it would seem, as Mr. Belloc has suggested, that his failure was due to an under-estimation or an unawareness of the forces against him. Not only Anne Boleyn, but every ambitious man also, was Wolsey's potential if not actual enemy.

In his adversity he is said, though with no

great assurance, to have proved an exemplary
Bishop. He was just and unbending to the lowly,
and rapidly gained their affection.

> ' *His overthrow heaped happiness upon him*
> *For, then, and not till then, he felt himself,*
> *And found the blessedness of being little,*
> *And, to add greater honours to his age*
> *Than man could give him, he died fearing God.*'

Not only that, there is reason to believe that at
times he also lived fearing God. There was nothing
mean about him, even in his vices. When he was
summoned from York on a charge of treason
(he had already been charged under the old
familiar *Praemunire*), he said that there lived not
on earth a man who could look him in the face
and charge him with untruth. He was ill with
dropsy and travelled but slowly and painfully.
He got no further than Leicester, where he died
at the Abbey of S. Mary de Prè. And it is said
that beneath his purple and fine linen, they found
a hairshirt on his back and upon his arm a ring of
iron.

His character has been a source of wrangling
ever since he began to lose the favour of the King.
Of the contemporary writers Erasmus, who enjoyed his patronage, praised him to that time and
then meanly joined in the common execration.
Polydore Vergil, whom he had once imprisoned,
abused him consistently. Whether he would have

H

fallen on the side of the angels, with Fisher and More, had he lived long enough, is a matter for conjecture. It seems at least probable that he would. There is an indication, in his behaviour and counsel to the King in his last sayings and his cryptic last message, that he had at last a firm mind on the point at issue, and a wholesome fear of God.

His ability and wisdom as an administrator and diplomat were rarely at fault. Whatever impression the probing of the post-Reformation pedants may have made upon his fame, he still stands a colossal figure with the large manner, whose ambition was the greatest asset his country possessed in his day.

He was the greatest of the ecclesiastical statesmen in England and the last of them. He achieved the complete combination of clerical and secular power, but used that power so improperly, for his own aggrandizement, neglecting the greater issues, that the combination could never occur again. He enriched himself so much at the expense of the Church, that others carried the process beyond its limit. In his intense preoccupation with his own state he missed the menace to the unity of the Church, the scaffolding of his eminence in England, when he was the one man who could have fought that menace with any chance of success.

X. LORENZO CAMPEGGIO

Lorenzo Campeggio, sometimes included amongst the English Cardinals because of his important participation in the affair of Henry's first divorce, was a native of Bologna, probably the most eminent jurist of his day, a good man, astute and firm of purpose. He was created Cardinal soon after Wolsey and made Cardinal-Protector of England, through whom English affairs at Rome passed, in the English interest. He held successively the Bishoprics of Hereford and Salisbury. His tactical procrastination in England in the matter of the divorce trial, the removal of the case to Rome, possibly at his suggestion, greatly exasperated the King and helped to provoke him to the breach with the Pope.

PART II. 1530–1930

ENGLAND IN SCHISM

CHAPTER IV

THE CLEAVAGE

I. JOHN FISHER

IN Cardinal John Fisher we find once again the type of scholar-priest who preceded the legal and political favourites of the last century. He rose in the Church not for his value to the King as a lawyer and a politician, nor for his royal connections. His piety and learning alone gained him honours and preferment. He rose in the end to higher dignity than any other English Cardinal, not excepting Nicholas Breakspear.

John Fisher came, like Thomas Wolsey, of a prosperous middle-class family. He was born and received his early education in Beverley, the ancient capital and Minster town of the East Riding of Yorkshire. From Beverley he went to Michael House, Cambridge, where in due course he graduated Master of Arts. By 1495 he had become Fellow, Proctor and two years later Master of Michael House. He had already a wide reputation for learning and sanctity. Having

taken orders he was chosen by Lady Margaret
Beaufort, Countess of Richmond and mother of
Henry VII, for her almoner, confessor and director.   In 1501 he proceeded Doctor of Divinity
and became Vice-Chancellor of the University.
He may have been tutor to the future Henry VIII
about this time.   For many years the young King
had a great respect for him.   Possibly by the influence of his patroness, but no less by his merits
and the recommendation of Bishop Foxe of Winchester, John Fisher received the Bishopric of
Rochester in 1504.   He was later offered richer
sees, but he preferred to retain this of Rochester,
the poorest in the kingdom, having in mind the
words of S. Paul, ' a bishop should be the husband
of one wife.'   Soon afterwards he was chosen
Chancellor of the University of Cambridge, an
office to which he subsequently received the unprecedented honour of election for life.

So far, his career had been the normal one for
a successful scholar in divinity.   As he rose he
used his position and influence in the patronage
of letters.   He invited Erasmus to Cambridge and
amongst his friends were Linacre, Grocyn, Dean
Colet and Sir Thomas More.   Presumably under
his direction, his patroness founded, in addition
to numerous lectureships, S. John's and Christ's
Colleges at Cambridge, and the Lady Margaret
Chairs of Divinity at Cambridge and Oxford,

BLESSED JOHN CARDINAL FISHER

Fisher being the first Professor at Cambridge in 1503. As Chancellor of Cambridge the Bishop ably fostered the Humanities, and especially the study of Greek. He was an exemplary Bishop in his diocese. Every writer of repute in his day bears testimony to his greatness. Vigorously and constantly he urged the need for reform in the Church, especially in the discipline and character of the clergy. No less vigorously did he oppose the reforms proposed by Luther and those whose doctrines were derived from Wycliff and the Lollards. He was nominated English representative at the Lateran Council in 1512, but did not go. It is more than likely that both he and Wolsey had a hand in the King's anti-Lutheran *Defence of the Seven Sacraments* which gained Henry the title of ' Fidei Defensor.'

On June 18, 1529, in the parliament chamber at the Black Friars there sat the Archbishop of York, Cardinal of S. Cecilia trans Tiberim, Thomas Wolsey, and the Cardinal Lorenzo Campeggio, Bishop of Salisbury, Archbishop of Bologna, legates of His Holiness Pope Clement VII, to judge whether it were lawful for the King to put away his wife. Beneath the Cardinal legates sat the chosen divines, scholars and lawyers of the realm, the Archbishop of Canterbury and many other bishops. On one side stood the counsel for the King, who were

Dr. Sampson, afterwards Bishop of Chichester, and Dr. Bell, afterwards Bishop of Worcester, with divers others. On the other side stood the counsel for the Queen, who were Dr. Fisher, Bishop of Rochester, and Dr. Standish, some time a Grey Friar, then Bishop of S. Asaph ; ' *in especial* ' (the chronicler tells us) ' *the Bishop of Rochester, a very godly man and a devout person.*'

The judges' Commission from the Pope being read openly the crier called out :

' King Henry of England, come into court ! ' whereupon the King answered, ' Here, my lords.' Then the crier called : ' Catherine, Queen of England, come into court,' who made no answer, but making obeisance to the Cardinals, pleaded for her wifehood and the honour of her children at the King's feet, having formerly objected to the court. She then rose and left the court escorted by her steward.

The King then rose, acquitted his wife of personal offence, and based his cause on his conscientious scruples, denying all amorous considerations. He demanded of the assembled prelates, in particular of his confessor, whether he did not do this on their advice and approbation, signified under their own seals. The Archbishop of Canterbury on their behalf assented : ' That is the truth if it please your Highness ; I doubt not but all my brethren here present will affirm the same.'

But that was not the truth. There was one man in the court who would affirm no such thing. Wherefore he stood forth and spoke : ' No, sir, not I ; ye have not my consent thereto.'

' No ! ha ! then ! ' quoth the King, ' look here upon this ; is not this your hand and seal ? ' and showed him the instrument with the seals.

' No forsooth, sire,' quoth the Bishop of Rochester, ' it is not my hand nor seal.' To that quoth the King to my lord of Canterbury :

' Sir, how say ye ? Is it not his hand and seal ? '

' Yes, sir,' quoth my lord of Canterbury.

' That is not so,' quoth the Bishop of Rochester, ' for indeed you were in hand with me to have both my hand and seal, as other of my lords had already done ; but then I said to you that I would never consent to no such act, for it were much against my conscience, nor my hand and seal should never be seen at no such instrument, God willing, with much more touching the same communication between us.'

' You say truth,' quoth my lord of Canterbury. ' Such words ye said unto me ; but at the last ye were fully persuaded that I should for you subscribe your name, and put to a seal myself and ye would allow the same.'

' All which words and matter,' quoth the Bishop of Rochester, ' under your correction, my lord, and supportation of this noble audience, there is no thing more untrue.'

' Well, well,' quoth the King, ' it shall make no matter, we will not stand with you in argument herein, for you are but one man.' And with that the court was adjourned to the next day of session.

So did John Fisher give the lie to the High Priest in the court of divines, where a better King might have been proud to own one just man. That day the Bishop of Rochester showed the courage of heart and strength of soul which would one day so shame the King that in his anger he would murder the Bishop.

Yet again before the same court, the truth and nothing but the truth was demanded by John Fisher. When it was beginning to be agreed that, in the matter of the Queen's marriage with the King's elder brother, long since dead, it was impossible to know the truth :

' Yes,' quoth the Bishop of Rochester. ' *Ego nosco veritatem*, I know the truth.'

' How know you the truth ? ' quoth my lord Cardinal.

' Forsooth, my lord,' quoth he. ' *Ego sum professor veritatis*, I know that God is truth itself, nor he never spake but the truth that saith, whom God hath joined together, let no man put asunder ; and forasmuch as this marriage was made and joined by God to a good intent, I say that I know, the which cannot be broken or loosed by the power of man upon no feigned occasion.'

The end of all this was, as everybody knows, that the case was transferred to Rome and the King could not get the divorce he sought from the Pope. So he made himself his own pope and got his divorce through his own Archbishop. Thomas Wolsey, his right hand and the right lobe of his brain, being dead, he behaved henceforth like a man half crazed.

It was not likely that John Fisher, of all men, would stand for this madness. It was nothing but great sorrow to him that his brother prelates, for fear or favour, gave their broken spiritual allegiance to the rampant King. He agreed that so far as the Succession was concerned, the realm might legalize whom it chose. But to make the King supreme Head of the Church there was no power, and to call him such was not the truth. He, John Fisher, *professor veritatis*, said so, and he knew the truth.

The King's weak weapons of deprivation, cruel imprisonment, torturous *procès verbal*, and the threat of death had no chance at all against the spirit of this man. From the time of the divorce trial before the Pope's legates, if not before, the Bishop of Rochester was a stumbling-block to the unlawful desires of the King. The King could not ignore John Fisher. The presence of sanctity is too embarrassing to the evil-doer, a curious psychological fact for which there are now many explanations, but the original one still holds good.

On June 17, 1535, the late Bishop of Rochester (for he had been deprived), but now Cardinal-priest of S. Vitalis (for he had been so created by Pope Paul III on May 21), appeared at the bar of the King's Bench before a common Middlesex jury of twelve, to answer the charge :

' That in the twenty-seventh year of King Henry's reign, he the said John Fisher, late Bishop of Rochester, had in the Tower of London, falsely, maliciously, and traitorously spoken and divulged against his due allegiance, before several of the King's true subjects the following words in English : That the King our sovereign Lord is not Supreme Head, on earth, of the Church of England.'

He had made the declaration to Rich, the King's man, who had asked his opinion for the quieting of the royal conscience ! He therefore maintained that he had not made the statement *maliciously* and was not in consequence guilty under the statute. All of which was true.

He was condemned to a traitor's death of hanging and butchering, but at the last moment the King relented, God help him, and ordered a clean cut with the axe. Thus died the man whose life, as the worthy historian Fuller says, could do the

King no hurt, whose life was not worth the King's while to take, since he was ' not only *mortalis* as all men, and *mortificatus*, as all good men, but also *moriturus*, as all old men, being past seventy-six years of age.'

This venomous and mean-spirited murder filled all the good and learned men of Europe with hatred and execration against Bluff King Hal.

For the King who had for years revered the Bishop as a father, the King who had boasted that no prince in Europe possessed a prelate equal in learning to the Bishop of Rochester, this King had seen fit to give the venerable old priest the death of a traitor, though, in fact, he succeeded only in giving him the death of a saint and martyr. John Fisher died as nobly as he had lived. His death was calm, dignified, holy : the perfect death of the just man. The multitudes were moved in the depths of their hearts, they beheld the strength of the Holy Ghost possessing the frail form of the man, and by that vision their Faith was renewed. The head of the saint, parboiled and stuck up on London Bridge, now wore not the mitre but the martyr's crown.

Cardinal John Fisher was beatified on the feast of S. Thomas of Canterbury, 1886. He lives as strongly now in the hearts of the faithful as he ever did. His works, however, are little read, it being the fashion to prefer translations of holy confessors from abroad. The works he composed in prison, *A Spiritual Consolation*, *The Ways of Perfect Religion*, and a *Treatise on the Necessity, Fruits and Method of Prayer*, and his sermons on the Penitential Psalms, preached at Rochester, are as fine spiritual English as can be found. Though other English Cardinals are more famous and many had a greater influence on affairs of State, their influence has died, while John Fisher's still lives. It has been objected against him that he was too blunt and truculent in the matter of the King's divorce, and that with tact he might have moved things otherwise. Those who make the objection miss the essential merit of that Yorkshire quality in his character by which he knew when not to dissemble, and did not.

II. REGINALD POLE

A year after the martyrdom of Cardinal John Fisher, Pope Paul III elevated to the Sacred College an Englishman, Reginald Pole, with the title of Cardinal-deacon of SS. Nereus and Achilleis. He was aged thirty-six and not yet a priest.

By his mother B. Margaret Pole, Countess of Salisbury, he was a royal Plantagenet and kinsman of Henry VIII, she being the granddaughter of Richard Duke of York and niece of Edward IV,

Henry's grandfather. She had been married, by Henry VII, to Sir Reginald Pole, K.G.

Reginald Pole was born at Castle Stourton, Staffordshire. He was educated at the school attached to the Charterhouse, at Sheen, and at Magdalen College, Oxford, under Linacre and Latimer. By virtue of his birth, he received many benefices whilst still a young man. Though not in orders he had probably received the tonsure. At his own request and by the King's consent he studied also at Padua, Rome, and later Paris. In 1527 he was made Dean of Exeter. His life during these years was that of an ecclesiastic and student, though he did not yet become a priest. His social position gave him wide facilities and many friends, and his abilities and character were respected and praised by such men as Erasmus and Sir Thomas More.

At the time of the affair of the trial of the King's first divorce case, he was conveniently at Paris. It has been said that the King sent him there to get the approval of the University. It is certain that he disapproved of the divorce proceedings. On Wolsey's death Henry offered him the Archbishopric of York, or if he preferred it, the fattest of all benefices, Winchester, now also vacant. Pole refused the bribes, and as soon as he could do so with discretion he obtained leave to return to Padua. The King's behaviour after the death of

Wolsey became very embarrassing for those of tender conscience who were not wholly with him. It may be assumed that Pole, up this to time, had not spoken his opposition too freely or too emphatically, though the King knew where his sympathies lay. Yet the King was still hopeful of gaining his kinsman's support and wrote to him in 1536 asking for his views on the divorce, thinking no doubt to get a favourable answer if only for family and diplomatic reasons. Pole not only expressed his absolute disapproval, but castigated Henry amply and solemnly for his behaviour in the matter, for his differences with Rome, and especially for the executions of Sir Thomas More and Cardinal John Fisher. After that he had the good sense to decline a singularly kind invitation to England to discuss the matter in a friendly way. Instead he went to Rome at the request of the Pope, to sit on a commission for the reform of Church discipline. He was made Cardinal-deacon at the end of the year.

He was now definitely and openly against the King, and for the Pope in his opposition. He committed himself entirely to the task of restoring the Church in England to its normal union with Rome and obedience to the Pope.

At the end of 1536, the people of the North rose in their anger at the dissolution of the monasteries. By the spring of 1537 the rising was very formidable, having its strength from Yorkshire and Northumberland which had been rich in religious houses and strong in the Faith since Roman times. The main rising was led by Robert Aske, a Yorkshire gentleman, though the whole rising was popular and spontaneous. The people bound themselves by oath to stand by each other, ' for the love which they bore to Almighty God, his Faith, the Holy Church and the maintenance thereof ; to the preservation of the King's person and his issue ; to the purifying of the nobility ; and to expulse all villein blood, and evil counsellors from his grace and privy counsel ; not for any private profit, nor to do harm to any private person, nor to slay or murder through envy, but for the restitution of the Church, and the suppression of heretics and their opinions.' This rising, the Pilgrimage of Grace, was eventually dispersed. The King, contrary to his express word, hanged and butchered the leaders freely afterwards.

The Pope saw in this rising an opportune occasion for publishing the Bull of excommunication and deposition prepared some time before (after the execution of Fisher and More), and he sent Cardinal Pole, as legate beyond the Alps, to give aid to the pilgrims, and to publish the Bull. He failed on account of the diplomatic difficulties occasioned by his passing through the territory of Francis I and Charles V. Needless to say,

Henry fulminated against his kinsman the Cardinal. Two years later when the legate had been sent by the Pope to make yet another attempt to join Francis and Charles against Henry, the King had judgment of treason pronounced against him, pursued him with spies, and, it is said, assassins to murder him. Meanwhile, though Henry could not catch the Cardinal, he could catch his relatives at home. These he persecuted mercilessly, executing most of them, including the Cardinal's saintly mother Margaret, Countess of Salisbury. The King kept her, his nearest kinswoman and a Plantagenet, over seventy years old, for two years in the Tower. He then had her beheaded. This noble woman refused to yield her head to the block, for, as she said, it had never committed treason—' if you will have it you must take it as you can,' and she had to be forcibly held down.

The King, whilst adhering strictly to the doctrines of the Catholic Church and imposing severe penalties on heretics, gloried in his rejection of papal authority. He had a mock naval battle in the Thames in which his ship fought the Pope's ship, captured it, and flung into the Thames effigies of the Pope and Cardinals, including his cousin Pole.

Meanwhile the Cardinal improved his position at Rome. In 1540 he was one of the three legates to open and preside over the Council of Trent.

He made no further move of any importance against the King.

On the death of Henry VIII and the accession of that monarch's son by Jane Seymour, Edward VI, Cardinal Pole made strenuous efforts to induce the Protector Somerset and the Privy Council to reconcile England with the Holy See. But the Protestant doctrines had gained too much strength in the English hierarchy and court. Too many already owed their position to the loot of the monasteries. Though there was no difficulty about ignoring the late King's wishes in other particulars, reconcilement with Rome was out of the question for the present.

Meanwhile Cardinal Pole remained at the papal court, and his position there was so high that when Paul III died in 1549, he very nearly succeeded him. By the influence of Cardinal Farnese he had obtained the requisite number of votes in the conclave. When, late in the evening, two Cardinals invited him to appear and be acclaimed Pope, he begged to be allowed to wait until the next morning, either from humility or fear of the office, or an inability to make up his mind. The next morning another Cardinal was proposed and elected Julius III.

In 1553, when Edward was dead and his half-sister Mary, daughter of Henry VIII and Catherine of Aragon, gained the throne, the suggestion that she should marry Cardinal Pole, as one of two eligibles, was defeated. His age alone was too much for Mary, and it is unlikely that the Cardinal himself had any inclination for married life. He had so far lived as an ecclesiastic, though he was not ordained, and except on the score of rank and family it is difficult to see how the suggestion of his marrying the Queen of England, daughter of Henry and Catherine of Aragon, could ever have been entertained. The other possibility, Courtenay, son of the Countess of Exeter, proved too much of a scamp. In due course she married Philip of Spain.

As the Catholic daughter of a Catholic father and mother she was resolved to keep England Catholic and stamp out the Protestantism which had gained a firm footing in high places, especially amongst the rich. For they, being mostly rich at the expense of the Church, saw a grave danger to themselves in any *rapprochement* with Rome. The nobility, old and new, had been enriched through Henry's dissolution of the monasteries and appropriation of Church revenues, and any restoration of their wealth to its former uses would be disastrous to them. They had strengthened their position under Edward VI, they had attempted to make Lady Jane Grey Queen. Mary, as Catherine's daughter, had naturally no sympathy with her father's defiance of the Pope, and she was bent on restoring the Faith, whole and entire, in communion with the Holy See. She began quietly enough. But the Protestants, who were strong in the City of London, were seriously alarmed, and Cranmer, who had pronounced her mother's marriage null, was still Archbishop of Canterbury. Open conflict could not long be delayed.

Mary's caution deleted all reference to papal authority or restoration of Church property in the early statutes which repealed the anti-Catholic legislation of her predecessor. The Pope appointed Cardinal Pole *legate a latere* to England, but Mary, advised that his arrival might cause trouble, warned him not to come nearer than Brussels.

After the suppression of Wyatt's rebellion and the marriage of Mary with Philip, the consequent strengthening of the Queen's position enabled the attainder against Cardinal Pole to be repealed. He was conducted to England with great pomp and formally received by the Chancellor, Philip and the Queen with ample and solemn ceremony. A motion for reunion with the Holy See was carried almost unanimously by both Houses, only two members of the Commons pluckily standing out. On the following day, the Cardinal legate formally absolved ' all those present, and the whole nation, and the dominions thereof, from all heresy and schism and all judgments, censures and penalties for that cause incurred ; and restored them to the communion of Holy Church, in the name of the Father, Son and Holy Ghost.'

Soon after this, the Cardinal published a decree protecting against interference or invalidation all ecclesiastical, charitable and educational institutions founded, all marriages contracted, all judicial processes made before ordinaries, and all transference of Church property during the schism. He had himself had scruples about confirming the alienation of Church property, but these had been removed by the Pope.

This should have satisfied all those who were fearful of their property, and they were the most numerous. Those whose consciences were worried about the restoration of papal authority, it was attempted to reassure by an Act which, among other things, carefully distinguished between civil and ecclesiastical jurisdictions, to a proper restriction of the latter. The practice and doctrines of the Faith and the unity of the Church in England with the Apostolic See were restored completely as they had existed in the twentieth year of Henry VIII, that is before the divorce.

Ambassadors were now despatched to the papal court. Before they arrived the Pope died, and there was a second attempt by Cardinal Farnese, supported by the King of France, to have Pole elected. But he was not quick enough. Nevertheless, Pope Marcellus II, who was unanimously chosen, died within three weeks, and there was yet a third attempt to make the English Cardinal Pope. Had he been in Rome instead of being legate in England, his presence might have secured the necessary support. At any rate, the attempt failed. It is doubtful whether the Englishman had the force of character, capacity for decision and resolution which were needed to make a successful Pope in his day, though he had learning and virtue enough.

The new Pope, Paul IV, at the instance of Pole, at once published a Bull by which at the petition of Mary and Philip Ireland was raised from a lordship to a kingdom. It was the English Pope, Adrian IV, who had given the lordship of Ireland to the King of England. The Irish, quite properly, maintained that this had been forfeited by the defection of Henry VIII from his allegiance to the Holy See. The new Bull improved the occasion.

It was not long after the marriage of Philip and Mary that the historical ill-fame of their reign was established by the burning of heretics. The majority of historians, and many contemporaries, acquit Cardinal Pole of active support of the persecutions. It is quite certain that he personally disapproved, and it was believed by some that the denunciation of such severity, made at its commencement by Philip's confessor, was inspired by

him. His confidential letter to the Cardinal of
Augsburg approves the penalty of death only in
extreme cases, in which the danger of the repetition
of errors is a menace to the faith of others ; and
even then every gentler remedy should be tried,
and the bishops should remember they are fathers
as well as judges. There is no definite evidence
that his conduct during the persecutions was not
in keeping with these counsels of lenity.

When Cranmer was deprived, before being
burnt for heresy, Cardinal Pole became the last
Catholic Archbishop of Canterbury. He had
already been ordained and raised to the dignity of
Cardinal-priest of S. Maria in Cosmedin. Contrary
to the suggestion which has naturally been made,
the Cardinal did not hasten Cranmer's death to take
his place but obtained respite for him several times.
Once deprived, Cranmer living was no greater
obstacle than Cranmer dead. As Archbishop
the Cardinal put an end to persecution in his
diocese and exerted himself to reform the clergy,
repair churches and re-establish Catholic practice.
His toleration and mildness even made him suspect of unorthodoxy in the eyes of the over-
zealous, and probably through pressure from these
(he does not seem to have had a strong character)
he issued a commission for the prosecution of
heretics in his diocese just before his death.

When Philip left the country, he left the Queen

in the care of the Cardinal, who though a member of the Council, hated politics and temporal affairs. He may not have been so obtuse in affairs of State as he appeared. Because he opposed the intrigues of the Spaniards who wished to make Philip absolute ruler, it was said (to a Spaniard) that he was no ' statesman, nor fit to advise or govern.'

The Pope, either believing Pole too moderate or for some diplomatic reason, cast suspicion on his orthodoxy, and after depriving him of his legateship would have recalled him to Rome. He did in fact create William Peto, Mary's Franciscan confessor, Cardinal, and transferred Pole's authority to him. But Peto, through Mary's action, did not know it. Philip and Mary protested vigorously against the action of the Pope, who even proposed calling Cardinal Pole to be examined by the Inquisition, but before matters proceeded further, the Cardinal was called Elsewhere.

He died on the same day as the Queen ; perhaps fortunately, for there was trouble brewing for him at Rome and Elizabeth disliked him strongly. Nevertheless, had he lived and been successful in his moderate counsels, Mary being dead, the history of England would have taken a very different turn. For Elizabeth was, as yet, a Catholic.

His chief defect seems to have been in force of

character. His influence would have been excellent could he have made it more effective. He was privately pious and publicly generous, merciful and charitable. He wore a remarkably fine beard and kept a good table, though he was himself ascetic.

III. WILLIAM PETO

On Easter Day 1532, William Peto, Franciscan Provincial of the Grey Friars, preached before Henry VIII at Greenwich. ' I am that Micheas whom thou wilt hate, because I must tell thee truly that this marriage is unlawful. I know that I shall eat the bread of affliction. . . .' And he did. The King, naturally enough, imprisoned him. When Thomas Cromwell, the King's bloodhound, remarked that Peto and Father Elston, his companion, deserved to be tied in a sack and thrown into the Thames, Peto replied, with a sarcastic smile (says Lingard) : ' Threaten such things to rich and dainty folk, which are clothed in purple, fare deliciously, and have their chiefest hopes in this world. We esteem them not. We are joyful that for the discharge of our duty we are driven hence. With thanks to God we know that the way to heaven is as short by water as by land, and therefore care not which way we go.'

The Friars Observants to which Peto belonged suffered severely under Henry. Like the Carthusians and the Brigittines, being withdrawn from the world and less corrupted with possessions than the more prosperous orders, they were less inclined to dissemble. They suffered considerable torture and starvation as well as the usual butchery at the end. The Friars Observants who did not die in confinement were banished to France and Scotland. Peto, after a spell of prison, went to Antwerp and stayed abroad until the accession of Mary. He was included in the Act of Attainder against Cardinal Pole and others in 1539.

He was the son of Edward Peto of Chesterton, Warwickshire, and Goditha, daughter of Sir Thomas Throckmorton. He was no doubt thereby related to Michael Throckmorton who was Cardinal Pole's secretary in Rome. He graduated Master of Arts at Cambridge in 1505 (Bishop John Fisher being Chancellor there), and at Oxford in 1510. He was one of the most learned men of his day, of exceptional holiness, a friend of Reginald Pole, John Fisher and Thomas More, the latter sending his books against Tyndale and Frith to Peto at Antwerp. He was, like his friends and all the best men of his day, fully alive to the grave abuses rampant in the Church, and he was far from averse to rigorous reform. But he was uncompromisingly opposed to Henry's claim to supremacy, and it is not surprising to learn from a letter written about him to Thomas Cromwell that he ' grew very hot in argument.' It was the day of hot argument, as many heretics learned under both Catholic and Protestant rulers. The same letter also said of Peto, that ' he could not flatter '—a rare compliment in those days.

In the year Henry died, 1547, the Pope gave Peto the Bishopric of Salisbury, not such a generous gift as it sounds, in the circumstances, for it was not until the accession of Queen Mary that he could return to England and take possession of the ravaged see. He then felt too old for the cares of a bishopric and resigned in order to retire to his old convent at Greenwich when Mary restored it. At this time he became Confessor to the Queen.

When Pope Paul wished to deprive Cardinal Pole of his legateship, some say because he was too lenient with heretics, he offered it to Peto, now eighty years old, creating him Cardinal for the purpose. The Pope said he had known Peto when he was in the family of Pole, and from the first he had determined to make him a Cardinal, considering him worthy of the honour both from his own knowledge and the testimony of others. It was natural that the Queen should object on Pole's account, and both the Cardinals were summoned to Rome. But death soon ended the difficulty for Peto and not long afterwards for Pole also.

For some strange and unexplained reason—possibly because Pole was more popular on account of his leniency, or because Peto was feared on account of his strong sentiments, or again because the idea of making such an infirm old man Cardinal and Legate appeared ridiculous to the mob —whatever the reason, it is on record that the saintly old man so late loaded with honours was regarded as a fit subject for jeering and mockery by the citizens of London, full as they were now of the enlightened spirit of a purer religion. He did indeed eat the bread of affliction, though he missed the martyrdom he seemed to court at the hands of Henry. He died probably in the spring of 1558 when the Queen and Cardinal Pole died.

IV. DAVID BEATON

Before Henry VIII divorced his first wife, Catherine, he had been willing that his nephew, James V of Scotland, should marry Princess Mary, his daughter by Catherine. But when he married Anne Boleyn, he saw in such a match the danger that James might dispute succession to the throne of England with the children of Anne, if any. Therefore he now decided against the match. He was greatly concerned to convert James to his view of the supremacy of rulers over the Church within their realms, and sent a treatise to him and a preacher also. The preacher, finding himself very unwelcome, wrote to Thomas Cromwell, referring to the Scots King's clerical counsellors as ' the Pope's pestilential creatures and the very limbs of the devil.'

The chief of these pestilential creatures was David Beaton or Bethune, a nephew of the Archbishop of S. Andrews, Primate and one time Chancellor of Scotland. He had been educated at S. Andrew's and Paris and was, amongst other things, Abbot of Arbroath (though not yet a priest) and Lord Privy Seal for Scotland. He acted as Scottish Resident at the French court, renewed the Scottish Alliance with France, and arranged the marriage of James V with the King of France's daughter Madeleine. When she died very soon after marriage, Beaton negotiated his King's marriage with Mary of Guise, who thus became the mother of Mary Queen of Scots.

Beaton was essentially a diplomat and statesman and a consummate intriguer, a man of courts rather than cathedrals. Nevertheless he collected eagerly such ecclesiastical perquisites as came his way, including the Bishopric of Mirepoix and later his uncle's primatial See of S. Andrew's. He was mainly responsible for the Scottish court's resistance to Henry VIII, and he had a great influence over the young King James and Francis I of France. Through their efforts on his behalf with Pope Leo Paul he was created Cardinal-priest of S. Stefano in Monte Celio on December 20, 1538. He succeeded his uncle soon after and became Chancellor of Scotland in 1543. David Beaton thus became the first Scottish Cardinal—the creation of Walter Wardlaw in 1381 notwithstanding, since it was the act of an anti-pope, Clement VII, whom Scotland supported, and it was therefore invalid.

Cardinal Beaton was a vigorous and uncompromising opponent of Henry, and this was in due course to lead to his violent end. Meanwhile his diplomacy kept Scotland reasonably independent and fairly free from interference. Henry's chief interference was by means of spies and preachers, as we shall see. That Henry feared and respected Beaton's abilities is clear from his tactics. It was when the Cardinal left Scotland for Rome, by way of France, presumably to form a league to carry out the Pope's deposition of the King of England, that King Henry seized the opportunity of treating with his nephew James alone. But James, probably forewarned, was not to be tempted into England. Henry's next weapon was war. Soon after the defeat of Solway Moss, and a week after the birth of his daughter the future Queen, James V died.

K

Whereupon Cardinal Beaton, now returned, published a will of the King, whereby he and three others were named regents during the infancy of the new Queen. The nobles, declaring this will a forgery, appointed the Earl of Arran regent and imprisoned the Cardinal on a charge of conspiring with the Duke of Guise against the Earl. By private treaty and the threat of an Interdict on Scotland by the Pope, he was released. With the support of Matthew Stewart, Earl of Lennox, he obtained possession of the Queen and forced Arran to come to terms, eventually uniting the nobles and the people against Henry. That King, in retaliation, did a little more ravaging and burning. But he failed to gain possession of the Queen from Beaton. The King's agents were now set to work against the Cardinal.

Beaton as Archbishop was anything but popular. His too vigorous persecution of heretics did not give him a pleasant character even with the faithful. It appears that there were several offers made to Henry to put an end to him for a consideration, but that consideration was not directly forthcoming, ' his highness not reputing the fact meet to be set forward expressly by his majesty, will not seem to have to do in it, and yet not mistaking the offer. . . .' But for a time apparently it was a case of money down or nothing done.

However, matters came to a head by another

route. George Wishart, a popular reformer-preacher, very likely an agent of Henry, was caught by Beaton, who had him hanged for sedition and burned for heresy. In addition to this the Cardinal had a private quarrel with Norman Leslie, Master of Rothes, about some property in Fife. The upshot was that Leslie and his father, the Earl of Rothes, Sir James Kirkcaldy and his son, Sir William, James Melville and several others conspired. With the result that the Cardinal-Archbishop, now *legate a latere* and Protonotary Apostolic, was murdered in his Castle of S. Andrew's one morning in 1546.

His personal life was far from blameless, though of late loyal Scots have sought to show that he was not so bad as he has been painted. Nevertheless, he was hardly a lovable character or an exemplary priest. His chief merit was in his capable, if not always very scrupulous, statesmanship and his firm and vigorous opposition to Henry VIII.

V. WILLIAM ALLEN

In the year 1554 when the attainder of Cardinal Pole was reversed and he came to England to support Queen Mary in the restoration of the Catholic Faith, there graduated Master of Arts at Oxford a Fellow of Oriel College, William Allen. He was the son of John Allen of Rossall, member of an ancient Lancashire family. Two years later he became principal of S. Mary's Hall and proctor, being now only twenty-four years old. On the death of Mary, the tide having once more turned strongly against the Faith in England, his position as a staunch Catholic became difficult, so he resigned all his preferments and went to Louvain. Within a year he returned to his native country, where he laboured to resist the persecution of Catholics and strengthen them against occasional conformity, since many at this time thought it a justifiable expedient to conform to the statutes which enforced outward participation in the established Protestant form of worship. Allen was a firm and uncompromising opponent of all dissembling in matters affecting the Faith. In 1565 he went abroad again and was ordained priest at Mechlin, where he lectured in theology. After a visit to Rome he proceeded to put into operation at Douay his plan for a Catholic University for Englishmen which should temporarily replace Oxford, as a sort of continuation, until the Faith should be re-established in England. It became in fact a seminary to provide priests for England. The missionary work was thus an afterthought, but it was most essential for replacing the priests who died, naturally and by the persecution, under Elizabeth. It is due to Allen's foundation and

WILLIAM CARDINAL ALLEN

his subsequent influence at Rome and with the Jesuits, that a supply of priests was kept up for the suffering Catholics, and the continuity of the Faith in England was maintained. Nearly a hundred priests were sent to England in the first five years of the College, and many of them suffered martyrdom. Allen was himself Professor of Divinity at the College.

It was on his appeal that the General of the Jesuits undertook to provide missionaries from the Society, and the two brilliant Englishmen, Edmund Campion and Robert Parsons, were sent. His efforts in Rome resulted in Gregory XIII's establishing the English College, and he was also the moving spirit in the foundation of the English College at Valladolid.

Allen was essentially an Englishman, and it was his patriotism as well as his faith which moved him to put all his efforts into the preservation of the Faith in England. It led him, on this account, to support Philip of Spain's proposed invasion. Philip, to prepare for the restoration of Catholicism in England, wanted a Cardinal-legate charged with the work, as Pole had been. He moved the Pope, Sixtus V, to elevate Allen, who had declined the honour under Pope Gregory. Hence the Englishman was created Cardinal-priest of S. Martin in Montibus on August 7, 1587, and though this promotion and its object were intended to be kept secret, it could not long remain so. The defeat of the Armada ended Philip's hopes in 1588, and the Cardinal was able to carry on as before in his academic labours in support of the missionaries to England. About this time he was nominated Archbishop of Mechlin, but he was never consecrated. He received the revenues of an abbey in Calabria and the Archbishopric of Palermo, but these were no more than the papal contribution to his maintenance and support. He was never a rich man.

His most enduring work, in the academic sphere, was done as Apostolic librarian under Pope Gregory XIV, when he undertook, with Cardinal Colonna, the revision of the Vulgate. With Dr. Bristow he was chiefly responsible for the English ' Douai ' version. He wrote very many tracts against Protestantism for circulation by the missionaries in England.

He was a man of unimpeachable character ; he is variously described as handsome and dignified, courteous and humble, learned and pious. He was to be the last Englishman in the College of Cardinals for a century. Though the next English Cardinal was to experience the lingering persecution, he lived to see the worst of it ended.

CHAPTER V

THE INTERVAL

I. PHILIP HOWARD

THIRTY-FIVE years after the death of Cardinal William Allen, the next English Cardinal was born in Arundel House, London—a Howard, the third son of Henry Francis Howard, third Earl of Arundel. This boy, Philip Thomas Howard, was thus great-grandson of Philip, first Earl of Arundel, who died for his Faith in the Tower and has since been beatified. On his mother's side the future Cardinal was a grandson of the Duke of Lennox and thus a kinsman of King Charles the First, then reigning.

He was educated at S. John's College, Cambridge (Cardinal John Fisher's foundation through his patroness Lady Margaret Beaufort). Possibly on account of the renewal of anti-Catholic activity towards the end of the reign of Charles I and during the ascendancy of the Puritans, he continued his education at Utrecht and Antwerp, entering the Order of Preachers and studying also at Naples and Rennes. He was ordained in 1652, at the age of twenty-three. His great enthusiasm was for the reconversion of England to the Faith for which his ancestor had suffered. He urged this work on the Chapter of the Dominicans at Rome, and his plea resulted in a decree laying upon provincials and priors the duty of making strong efforts to obtain British novices. In 1657 he founded a Priory at Bornhem in East Flanders and was made first Prior.

It was shortly after this that he appeared somewhat furtively upon the stage of English affairs. In 1659 he was in England on a secret mission in the cause of Charles II, and had to leave hurriedly, the Polish Ambassador smuggling him out of the country in the disguise of a Polish servant. Once back at Bornhem he proceeded with his plan for a school for training Dominican missionaries for England.

It was but reasonable, considering his efforts for the restoration, that Charles II should think highly of him. Hence in 1662 we find him at Portsmouth as a witness to the King's Catholic marriage to Katherine of Braganza. He was the new Queen's first chaplain and became her Grand Almoner, residing at S. James with what was then the very comfortable salary of £500 a year.

The religious vacillations of the King and the tactless zeal of his Catholic brother, the Duke of York and future James II, maintained a state of

unrest and disquiet in religious matters. The
consequent nervousness ended in panic and persecution, which made Philip Howard's position
doubly difficult. James became an open Catholic
about 1670, and by 1672, the restoration of the
Catholic hierarchy being in the air, Howard was
nominated Vicar-Apostolic with a bishopric *in
partibus*. Not only were the anti-Catholic faction
now very apprehensive, but the Catholic chapter
in England also resented the appointment. They
claimed a traditional right to nominate their own
bishop, though they had apparently no personal
objection to Philip Howard. The Pope conceded
their point, but, what with the anti-Catholics on
the one hand and the Catholics on the other,
Howard found his position in England too un-
comfortable. He returned to his Priory at Bornhem in 1674.

The next year he was created by Pope Clement
X Cardinal-priest of S. Cecilia trans Tiberim
(Wolsey's title), afterwards exchanging the title
for that of the Dominican church of S. Maria
super Minervam.

As part of his activities on behalf of the Church
in England, he secured that the feast of S. Edward
the Confessor was made universal. He rebuilt
the English College at Rome and prepared new
rules for Douai College, Cardinal Allen's foundation. From 1679 he was Cardinal-protector of

England and Scotland. He always opposed the precipitate methods of James, Duke of York and later King, in religious matters, and the end of the persecution might have come sooner, with less handicap to English Catholics, had his counsel won the day. As it was, he lived to see the end of the extreme persecution in England, the last martyr dying in 1681. He was always a strong Royalist and supporter of the Stuarts—he gave a great feast and had an ox roasted whole in Rome to celebrate the birth of an heir to James II. Amongst his friends were the three Catholic sons of John Dryden, one of whom, Thomas, he attracted to the Dominican Order.

Titus Oates, who would swear anything, swore that Cardinal Howard was a party to the Popish plot, but though he was impeached for treason, the Cardinal could afford to take the matter calmly, being resident in Rome where the King's writ could not run.

He died in 1694 and was buried in his titular church.

II.   HENRY STUART

Thirty years after the death of Cardinal Howard, who had seen James II put an inglorious end to the reign of the Stuarts in England, a grandson of James was born in Rome, and christened Henry

Benedict Maria Clement Stuart. His father was the Old Pretender, the Chevalier de S. George (to Jacobites, James III), and his mother was the daughter of Prince James Sobieski. He had an elder brother, Charles Edward, the Young Pretender, later the Jacobite Charles III. When Charles Edward made the romantic and forlorn attempt to regain the throne of his ancestors and raised the standard of James III in the " Forty-five," Henry Benedict was with him. After the glorious failure of that attempt, which ended with the defeat at Culloden and the butchery of the clans by the Duke of Cumberland, George II's son, he returned to Rome to enter the priesthood. His family, being the Catholic hope of dynastic opposition to the Protestant and German Georges, was naturally in a special position at Rome. Henry was twenty-two when he received the tonsure in 1747, and within six months he was Cardinal-deacon of S. Maria in Campitelli, priest, and Cardinal-priest of the Holy Apostles. As younger son of the Old Pretender he was Duke of York and known as the Cardinal of York. Before long he was Bishop of Ostia, Arch-priest of the Vatican Basilica and Cardinal Camerlengo. On the accession of Pope Clement XIII he became titular Archbishop of Corinth, and in 1761 Cardinal-Bishop of Frascati. In 1788, on the death of his brother Charles Edward, Charles III, he became titular

King Henry IX of Great Britain, France and Ireland.

But though he used the royal title and style as the last of the Stuarts, he was not made of the stuff of his father and brother. He was far less of a king and a ruler than a genial and amiable scholar. At the flood of the Revolution, the French poured into Frascati and sacked it, the royal Cardinal being driven first to Padua and then to Venice. He had lost the revenues of his French benefices, he could not now collect those of Frascati, and his other resources he had expended in aid of the Pope. In his distress he was granted, and he accepted, an annuity from George III, his rival on his throne. In return he bestowed the Crown jewels, retained by James II, upon the Prince of Wales, Beau Nash's fat friend and the future George IV, so acknowledging the establishment of the German dynasty which had supplanted his own. He spent the rest of his life a patron of art and letters, forming a fine collection of art treasures and a good library. He became Dean of the Sacred College, and in 1803 he died at Frascati. With him closed the male line of the royal Stuarts. That line which his brother strove to end in a blaze of glory, he ended in a warm glow of refinement. He was buried in Rome beside James III and Charles III, and the great Canova made his monument.

III. Charles Erskine

Just before the Cardinal of York died, another Scotsman was raised to the purple, Charles Erskine, son of a Scottish father Colin, of the family of the Earls of Mar and Kellie, and Agatha Gigli, an Italian. Under the patronage of his countryman, the Cardinal of York, he was educated at the Scots College and became an ecclesiastical lawyer. He was Doctor of Laws in 1770, being then thirty-one. Twelve years later he was Pro-Auditor and Promoter of the Faith, and in 1783 he was domestic prelate, Canon of S. Peter's and Dean of the College of Consistorial Advocates. Up to this time he had not taken more than minor orders, perhaps not more than the tonsure, but with advancement and benefices in view he was ordained sub-deacon.

From 1793 to 1801, Erskine was Papal Envoy in England. His position was one of extreme delicacy. In Ireland the Catholics had just obtained the vote, though they still suffered severe penalization. In England, towards the end of his stay especially, more intelligent opinion, such as that led by Sydney Smith in the *Edinburgh Review*, was favouring the abolition of religious persecution and the complete enfranchisement and emancipation of Catholics. But the "No-Popery" cries were loud and insistent, and the position was not eased by the danger of alliance between Irish Catholics and the French for the purpose of invasion. The Catholic question was one for political intrigue rather than speedy settlement on just lines. The King, Farmer George, was a stubborn bigot. His ministers were not much better, though it is true that they blew both hot and cold in the manner of their kind. Even the Catholics, who had suffered so much and become so closely knit in adversity, were a difficulty in themselves. They had suffered severance from the Holy See and developed a social autonomy. They had at times felt keenly the neglect of the Holy See. They had become homogeneous and independent-minded. As we we have seen, a century ago they had objected to the appointment of Cardinal Howard from Rome. Their lot had improved but little in a hundred years, and consequently they needed careful handling. It is a singular tribute to Erskine that he managed this business of papal envoy with sufficient skill and tact to improve relations between England and the Papacy, and there is no doubt that he advanced the cause of Catholic emancipation in this way.

He returned to Rome in 1801 and soon after was created Cardinal-deacon of S. Maria in Portico. He was an intimate of Pope Pius VII and imprisoned with him in the Quirinal when the French invaded Rome. He was allowed to go free, whilst the Pope was kept in custody. Yet having lost all his possessions by the invasion, he was destitute but for the help of his Protestant relatives and friends.

In 1809 Napoleon ordered him, now seventy years old, to go to Paris and stay there. He died in 1811 and was buried in what is now the Pantheon but was then the Church of Ste. Génevière.

IV. THOMAS WELD

As the more severe forms of religious persecution were eased under the succeeding Georges, in an England now overwhelmingly Protestant, a few of the older Catholic families began to recover their social status, and those which had retained a basis of property and capital began to re-establish their fortunes. Though legally and politically ostracized they could use their talents and such capital as they possessed to secure a share in the fruits of commercial and imperial development, which were pretty well one and the same thing. Under the reigning and swelling oligarchy, wealth, whether inherited, developed, or newly acquired, was a sufficient pass-key to social eminence. Thus it is that we find the old Catholic family of Weld entertaining His Bucolic Majesty King George III at their ancestral castle of Lulworth in Dorset, and gaining the favour of that exemplary bigot.

The heir to Lulworth, Thomas Weld, was born in London in 1773. As befitted his family and Catholic traditions he married, in 1798, a granddaughter of Lord Clifford, whose family was also dynastically loyal to the Faith. She died three years later, leaving him a daughter. When the girl married, in the year of Waterloo, Thomas, having now no family liabilities, resigned his estates to his brother Joseph and entered the priesthood. He was ordained at Paris in 1821, being then forty-eight. Joseph Weld continued to dispense the hospitality of the family and maintain its position in the society of his day. He was one of the first to build racing yachts. So far as the Church was concerned the family was foremost in befriending the religious driven from France during the Revolution. It was with the consent of Thomas, as heir, that his father had given the mansion of Stonyhurst to the Society of Jesus, thus enabling the foundation of the College which was to play such an effective part in the resuscitation of the Faith in England.

It was natural that with such credentials Thomas Weld's career in the Church would not fail for want of notice. Soon after his ordination he spent some five years on parochial work in

London. In 1826 he was named coadjutor-Bishop of Kingston, Upper Canada, and consecrated Bishop of Amycla *in partibus* at S. Edmund's, Ware. He never went to Canada, but after some delay took his sick daughter to Rome, where in 1830 he was created Cardinal-priest of S. Marcellus. This was a wise and appropriate, though not necessarily direct, sequel to the passing of the Emancipation Act. From this time he remained in Rome, living in the Odescalchi Palace, where his personality made a rendezvous for the best of Roman society, native and foreign. It was here in the Lent of 1835 that Nicholas Wiseman delivered his lectures ' On the connection between Science and Revealed Religion.' Cardinal Weld died in 1837 and was buried in the Church of S. Mary Aquiro. Wiseman, the future Cardinal, preached his funeral oration.

One of the most important things Thomas Weld did concerning the revival of the Church in England, and therefore affecting the history of England, was to befriend and support Bishop Milner in his critical conflict with the Catholic Committee in 1813. Milner as Vicar-Apostolic of the western district at this important time was a wise and learned priest with a full sense of his responsibilities. Fortunately he had the requisite courage to maintain his views. Not only did he find it necessary to persist in uncompromising opposition

L

to the Government in the matter of the oath of allegiance in the Catholic Relief Bill of 1791 (which he made them cut out), and in the matter of the Government's claim to veto the appointment of Catholic bishops, but he found himself in consequence of these and other matters opposed by the whole of the Catholic Committee. He would hardly have survived this last, a more serious difficulty, had he not received the loyal support of a man in so influential a position as Thomas Weld.

V. CHARLES ACTON

The next Englishman to follow Cardinal Weld in the Sacred College, Charles Januarius Edward Acton, revived the long-lapsed tradition of English distinction in ecclesiastical law. He had considerable influence on the position of the Church in England, and made a significant visit to England in the year of the Catholic Emancipation Act. He was in general charge of English affairs at the Vatican in the last ten years of his life, especially after the death of Cardinal Weld. He was created Cardinal-priest of S. Maria della Pace within two years after Weld died, though the fact was not proclaimed for a further three. The gaps in English representation in the College of Cardinals are now appreciably shortened, and very soon we are as well represented there as in the heyday of Catholic England. The point appears small, but it is significant both as indicating the reviving importance of the English at Rome and the expansion of papal policy. It was due to Cardinal Acton, no doubt supported by Wiseman, that in 1839-40 the Church in England was divided by Gregory XVI into eight vicariates-apostolic as a prelude to the restoration of the English hierarchy ten years later.

Acton was an Englishman by family and education, but he was born in Naples, whence his Christian name of Januarius, after the patron of that city. His father, Sir John Francis Edward, was a prosperous merchant who held prominent posts in the Neapolitan kingdom under Ferdinand IV, being at various times Premier, War Minister and Finance Minister. His family, like that of Cardinal Wiseman, was one of many distinguished Catholic families which had been driven out of the British Isles during the persecutions and established themselves on the continent. Sir John had been born at Besançon, where his father practised as a physician. It is of such stock that men of great ability most commonly arise. They are the backbone of any society wherein they flourish. Charles Acton's father, still very much an Englishman, though he was scorned by England and welcomed by Naples, sent Charles to school in England. He passed through the English gentleman's mill, Westminster School and Magdalene College, Cambridge, and was no worse for it. His Faith had been too well planted to suffer from the younger Protestant culture. At twenty he entered the Accademia Ecclesiastica. He soon showed unusual talent and won the esteem of successive Popes. Leo XII made him Chamberlain and attaché to the Paris Nunciature. Pius VIII made him vice-legate at Bologna. After his visit to England in Emancipation Year, 1829, he was made Assistant Judge in the Roman civil court by Gregory XVI, and in 1837, the year Cardinal Weld died, he became auditor to the Apostolic Chamber, being probably the first Englishman to hold the office. His importance in the Curia may be gauged from the fact that he acted as interpreter and sole witness at the momentous interview between Pope Gregory XVI and Czar Nicholas I. His association with the developments in England at this time have already been mentioned and they were of special significance. Hence his death at the early age of forty-four was a great loss to the Church in this country. He was a man of singular quality of mind, diplomat, musician and wit, and had a reputation for generosity. He declined the Archbishopric of Naples, his native town, where he died in 1847.

NICHOLAS CARDINAL WISEMAN

CHAPTER VI

THE SECOND SPRING

I. NICHOLAS WISEMAN

THIS story, now reaching the first Cardinal-Archbishop of Westminster, comes closer to our own day. There are men and women now living who might remember the death of Cardinal Wiseman, though there must be very few indeed who can remember the furore which followed his appointment in 1850.

The restoration of the hierarchy, foreshadowed by the increase in vicars-apostolic some ten years before, was bound to rouse Protestant England. It is true that for a long time, ever since the repeal of the Penal Laws, Catholic bishops and priests had ministered to the faithful in increasing numbers, and that openly. Nevertheless their paucity and poverty, if nothing else, ensured that so far as the bulk of the public was concerned they were comparatively obscure. The operations at the Vatican of successive Englishmen such as Cardinals Weld and Acton, the missionary activities of the vicars-apostolic and the work of the Catholic Committee, interested very few beyond themselves.

But the restoration of the hierarchy was quite another matter. It was a distinct formal act of the Papacy, a thing the public could recognize as such though they might not understand it, and therefore an event full of possibilities as political capital. The significant matter was the naming of English sees after English towns instead of giving the English bishops titular sees *in partibus infidelium* as before.

To comply with the Emancipation Act, the titles might not clash with those of the prelates of the Elizabethan establishment ; otherwise there was no legal objection, or indeed any at all for reasonable men at a reasonable time.

It so happened that neither the men nor the times were as reasonable as they might be. There was a certain public alarm, for the public was strongly Protestant, at the Tractarian movement and the conversions consequent upon it. The movement had been given wide publicity by its opponents, who had raised the ' No Popery ! ' cry very loudly in their panic. The conversion of Dr. John Henry Newman occurred in 1845, and it had been followed by a steady leakage to Rome. Controversies were both bitter and loud. This business had continued just long enough to create

a very unfavourable atmosphere, when the decisive step was taken in 1850. The 'No Popery'
propagandists gave one loud chorus of 'We told
you so!' and the public was once more ready to
believe, with the Reverend Abraham Plymley, 'that
the Pope was hovering round the coast in a fishing
smack, that he had landed and been hid at S.
Albans by the Dowager Lady Spencer, or that
he had dined privately at Holland House.' The
creation of an Archbishopric of Westminster was
certainly audacious under these conditions. The
temper of the public, which burnt effigies of the
Pope and the new Archbishop, clamouring for a
restoration of the penal laws against Catholics,
created an unpleasant situation and a difficult task
for the new Metropolitan. This was made worse
by serious differences within the fold, such as we
have referred to in the case of Bishop Milner. It
is possible, since he is credited with having urged
the Pope to this move, that he had only himself
to blame. In any case, the step once resolved upon,
Dr. Wiseman was the obvious man for the hour.
His learning, great ability and influence at Rome,
his English character, his acquaintance with the
English clergy, made him so. He had had great
influence on the Oxford Movement, Newman and
Hurrell Froude having been to Rome to consult
him. He had been President of Oscott Seminary
when the Movement was at its height; he had

been coadjutor to the Vicar-Apostolic of central England, and at Rome he had been successively vice-rector and rector of the English College. Few could be better acquainted with the field of operations, few equalled him in power of intellect.

Hence, despite the ugly situation and even the heavy criticism which followed his handling of it, he lived down the furore and remained for fifteen years in the see, consolidating the new organization. His title, by the way, was that previously held by Boso Breakspear, of Cardinal-priest of S. Pudentiana.

Nicholas Patrick Stephen Wiseman came of an Irish family in exile, his father being a merchant in Spain. He was born at Seville in 1802, and his mother consecrated him to the service of the Church by laying him as a child upon the high altar of Seville Cathedral. He was educated at Ushaw College, where John Lingard was his master, and they became close friends.

It may be observed in passing that Lingard has been claimed to be a Cardinal, but at the best there is a suggestion of a doubtful creation *in petto* which was never proclaimed. Lingard was never referred to as Cardinal, and never performed any of the functions of a Cardinal. That he was worthy of the honour we need not doubt ; his scholarship and great labours as a historian, culminating in his

History of England, were very fair qualification, as qualification goes, for such an office. His history was jibed at as being contrary to all the accepted history in his day, and in so far as it gave the lie to the current Protestant versions of history, rarely supported by references to manuscripts, the jibe was just and the offence praiseworthy. Lingard drew very largely on original contemporary sources for his history, taking as little as possible second-hand. The labour of this and providing the accurate references with which his work abounds was arduous and eminently rewardable. The history has been freely used in compiling this present account of the Cardinals.

To return to Wiseman. After his English education and fortunate contact with the great mind of Lingard, he went to the English College, Rome, being ordained at twenty-three. He rapidly distinguished himself in oriental scholarship, publishing his researches as *Horae Syriacae*, assisting in the compilation of a Syriac Grammar, and being elected professor-supernumerary in Hebrew and Syro-Chaldaic at the Roman Archigymnasium of the Sapienza. On his return to England he helped to found the *Dublin Review*, and in 1840, the year in which he became president of Oscott, he was consecrated Bishop of Melipotamus *in partibus*, being now thirty-eight. In 1848 he was diplomatic envoy from Pope Pius IX to the Prime

Minister Palmerston, and then stepped successively from pro-Vicar-Apostolic of the London district to Vicar-Apostolic and Metropolitan. When the storm broke it found Palmerston, though weakly, on the Catholic side, and his opponents, led by Lord John Russell, crying, ' No Popery.'

The only outcome of the Palmerston-Russell fight, the weapon which was to drive away the bogey of Popery and let good Protestants sleep peacefully, was an abortive Ecclesiastical Titles Bill, forbidding Catholics to take their titles from places within the United Kingdom. It was ignored by the hierarchy, never put into operation, and quietly repealed twenty years later.

Cardinal Wiseman's literary work other than that already noted includes *Fabiola, or the Church of the Catacombs*, still popular with Catholic readers, and *Recollections of the last Four Popes*, all of whom he had known when at Rome. He preached and lectured extensively. Robert Browning, the poet, satirized him in the heavy manner in *Bishop Blougram's Apology ;* the satire was neither very just nor very effective. Most of Browning's admirers would prefer even *Sibrandus Schafnaburgensis*, but that, like truth, is at the bottom of the well. No doubt it amused Browning as well as Wiseman, who reviewed it generously, as he could afford to do.

HENRY EDWARD CARDINAL MANNING

II. HENRY EDWARD MANNING

In the second quarter of the nineteenth century, preceding the restoration of the hierarchy in England, there arose in the Church of England a movement towards the restoration of Catholic doctrine in the Elizabethan establishment, independent of communion with the See of Rome. Ever since the Reformation there had been clergymen in the Anglican Church who regarded Protestantism as heresy whilst rejecting the supremacy of the Holy See. Such rejection, it must be remembered, had been made legally compulsory. Even many Catholics in the time of Henry and Elizabeth had believed that it was morally expedient to take the Oath of Supremacy. In a parallel manner many who took the Oath of Supremacy and subscribed to the Thirty-nine Articles of the Elizabethan establishment, believed that the Church of England, though newly organized and State-controlled, was still continuous with the pre-Reformation Church, doctrinally and sacramentally. It must not be forgotten that Henry VIII was always a Catholic in doctrine, never Protestant.

The Anglican Church, during more than two centuries of persecution of those who held Catholic doctrines, was under a nominal Protestant Head personated in later times by the very Protestant

German Georges, supported by a Protestant Government influencing and controlling the disbursement of benefices. It was natural that it should become permeated with Protestant doctrine. When to hold an opinion in the Catholic direction was dangerous, thinking in a Catholic direction was futile. But as persecution relaxed, and the religious atmosphere was less oppressive, it was inevitable that the thoughts of those in the ancient seats of learning should wander in the direction of the ancient Faith. They were living in its buildings, using its libraries, reading its manuscripts. Thus the gradual growth of toleration, culminating in the Emancipation Act of 1829, led easily to the enquiry towards the ancient Faith and practice known as the Oxford Movement.

The most notable event in this movement was the conversion of John Henry Newman to Catholicism, whole and Roman. The crisis of his position occurred with the wholesale condemnation of his Tract in which, following the policy of the rest of the movement in maintaining that their Catholicism was anything but Roman, he tried to show that the Thirty-nine Articles were not irreconcilable with Catholic doctrine, though opposed to Roman errors and dogma. If this were so, Anglican clergymen could be ' Catholics ' (not of course in communion with Rome) and subscribe with an easy conscience to the Articles. The tract was vigorously condemned by the Anglican hierarchy and many leading clerics, even those associated with Newman in the movement. One of them was Henry Edward Manning, Archdeacon of Chichester. This was in 1841. He was to be the first of the converts of the Oxford Movement to gain admission to the College of Cardinals.

Manning was thoroughly English, of a typically representative upper middle-class family in the English oligarchy. His father was Governor of the Bank of England and a Member of Parliament. Born in 1808 at Totteridge, Herts, he passed through the process proper to his class, Harrow, Balliol and the Colonial Office.

But after two years in Whitehall he changed direction and returned to Oxford to take Anglican orders. The date is 1832, when the Oxford Movement was taking definite form. Manning became Fellow of Merton, was ordained, obtained successively the curacy and rectorship of Woolavington-cum-Graffham, and was married before the end of 1833.

In the year 1837, in which his wife died, he was made rural dean, and within a few years Archdeacon of Chichester and select preacher at Oxford. He was now, at thirty-four, a pillar of the Establishment. He opposed Tract XC, as we have seen, and preached an anti-papal sermon on Guy Fawkes day, the traditionally favourite day for that exercise.   Nevertheless he was no Protestant. He wrote on *The Unity of the Church*, an exposition of Anglo-Catholic principles which might be called his ' tract ninety.' As one active in the Movement he voted against the degradation of William George Ward by the Oxford Convocation for heresy, in the year of Newman's conversion. The position was now thoroughly alarming the Anglican Church and such of the public as were sufficiently interested.

Manning went abroad and in his travels visited Pope Pius IX. On his return two things happened which vitally affected his future. The first was the Gorham judgment, the second the restoration of the hierarchy. Early in 1850 a High Church bishop refused to induct to a living a clergyman who explicitly denied the doctrine of baptismal regeneration. The clergyman appealed to the judicial committee of the Privy Council and obtained judgment against the bishop.

Now came the crisis for Manning. Here was a body of lay lawyers defining the dogmas of the Church of England on the Sacrament of Baptism and declaring against its sacramental character. This was the natural consequence of subjecting the Church to the State, with the King nominally head of the Church in spiritual matters. It was too much for many Anglican clergymen, especially the Anglo-Catholics of the Oxford Movement.

Dr. Manning was one of them. He wrote against the judgment and the jurisdiction of the Crown in *The Appellate Jurisdiction of the Crown in Matters Spiritual*, resigned the Archdeaconry of Chichester and became a Catholic. In nine weeks he was ordained priest. After a course of studies at Rome he returned to become Provost of the new Westminster Chapter and establish the Oblates of S. Charles. He was soon involved in numerous controversies, in the course of which he vigorously defended the papal temporal power.

When Cardinal Wiseman died, the Pope appointed Manning to succeed him as Archbishop of Westminster, despite the opposition of the English Chapter. There is no doubt that the choice was influenced not only by his reputation and ability, but by his enormous industry and dominating energy added to strong ultramontane views. Though his family influence may have operated to gain him advancement in the Church of England, it can have had very little effect at Rome. A strong active archbishop with brains was required at Westminster, and here was the man. One of his first acts was to establish the Westminster Education Fund—he was strongly opposed to State aid for elementary education, and in view of the educational difficulty over government grants and the admission of religious instruction to-day, his opposition was almost prophetic.

Archbishop Manning served on the Committee *de Fide* at the Vatican Council 1869–70. He defended the doctrine of papal infallibility vigorously against its opponents in the Church and in England, notably W. E. Gladstone, who had been his friend at Oxford. His work on the subject, *Petri Privilegium*, was published in 1871. In 1875 he was created Cardinal-priest of SS. Andrew and Gregory on the Cœlian Hill.

In 1878 Cardinal Manning assisted at the election of Pope Leo XIII, to whose famous encyclical, *Rerum Novarum*, on behalf of the labouring classes, he is said to have contributed much. He was in fact very popular in England for his work for the poor and his sympathy with the working classes in their struggle for reasonable conditions and wages. He was friendly with many labour leaders and with Edward Prince of Wales, and he personally intervened in the Dock Strike of 1889. He sat on Royal Commissions on the housing of the poor and on the Education Acts.

Modern biographers have made much capital out of the differences between Manning and Newman and the former's treatment of the latter before Newman was made Cardinal. Manning has been pictured as an astute and ambitious schemer, and Mr. Lytton Strachey, for example, has made him another Bishop Blougram. All this may be good saleable biography, but it is not necessarily true.

JOHN HENRY CARDINAL NEWMAN

The issues are almost too recent for safe judgment to be passed, but the fact remains that Cardinal Manning, ambitious or not, served the Church and his country with great energy and to good purpose, and he was a powerful and popular influence on the England of his day.

He died in 1892 and now lies in the Cathedral Church of Westminster.

III. JOHN HENRY NEWMAN

John Henry Newman was a very different manner of man. His origins and training were not dissimilar from Cardinal Manning's, though perhaps Newman started with a greater anti-Roman bias, his father being probably of Dutch Protestant extraction and his mother, Jemima Fourdrinier, being of a well-known Huguenot family. He was born in 1801, educated at Dr. Nicholas's School, Ealing, and Trinity College, Oxford. He was successively Fellow of Oriel College, Curate of S. Clement's, Oxford, vice-Principal of S. Alban's Hall, Whitehall preacher, and Vicar of S. Mary the Virgin, Oxford, by 1828, being now twenty-seven. So far he had made the normal progress of an exceptionally brilliant Anglican clergyman.

In 1832 he visited Rome with Richard Hurrell

M

Froude, and the Oxford Movement took definite shape on his return. He was the leading figure of the Movement and strongly anti-Roman. He persistently maintained the Catholic character of the Anglican Church *independent of Rome*. His Tract XC of *Tracts for the Times* ended this phase of his career. Though written, as we have seen, to reconcile the holding of Catholic doctrines with acceptance of the Thirty-nine Articles, it was universally condemned as ' Roman.' The submission of the author to the Holy See which followed, was therefore an event of disastrous import to the State Church of England and greatly strengthened the position of the Catholic Church in this country. This occurred in 1845. It was the signal for the outbreak of a ' No-Popery ' ramp on the one hand, and on the other the secession of many prominent Anglicans to Catholicism during subsequent years. It expedited, at least, the restoration of the Catholic hierarchy in England.

Newman's prolific writings, instinct with scholarship and great intellectual power, were almost wholly concerned with the very difficult task of maintaining an unstable position. The *Via Media* was very much like a tight-rope, and the spectator, marvelling at the skill of the walker, sooner or later suspects that there is a catch in it. Hence it was impossible for Newman to escape the charge of intellectual dishonesty, since he walked into the Church of Rome not even backwards, but whilst ostensibly walking away from it. There had of course been compromises, like the tricks of balance to which the tight-rope walker resorts. This fact gave strength to the attacks of his critics. These attacks continued for many years and culminated in charges of plain dishonesty, such as that Newman did not consider truth a necessary virtue, made by Charles Kingsley. Newman's reply was a comprehensive history of his religious opinions—*Apologia pro Vita Sua*, his greatest work, now reckoned one of the masterpieces of literature.

Meanwhile from his conversion, he wrote and lectured with great industry and effect. He published in 1845, the year of his conversion, *An Essay on the Development of Christian Doctrine*, and in the following year he was ordained priest and created Doctor of Divinity in Rome. In his stalwart fight against the ' No-Popery ' turmoil which developed enormously after 1850, he suffered conviction and fine for libel for justly exposing an apostate adventurer, an Italian ex-priest, who was one of the prime assets of the ' No-Popery ' faction.

From 1854 to 1858 he was rector of Cardinal Cullen's projected Catholic University of Ireland, but the political difficulties, civil and ecclesiastical, made the position untenable.

Probably the most tangible result of his efforts in Ireland is the essays *On the Idea and Scope of a University* and *The Rise and Progress of Universities*. He returned to Edgbaston, Birmingham, where he had established the Oratory when he came back from Rome. In 1864 appeared the *Apologia*. In 1870, though he doubted whether the definition of papal infallibility was opportune, he assented to it completely, since he had held and taught the doctrine 'long before the Vatican Council was dreamed of.' But in this as in many other things it was almost inevitable that a man of his genius and his temperament should be misunderstood and misinterpreted by his contemporaries within the Church as without; this had been his lot from his earliest Anglican days. It was not until he was nearly eighty that he ceased to be a figure of controversy and his greatness in philosophy and literature was publicly recognized. In 1877 he was elected Honorary Fellow of Trinity College, Oxford. Two years later he accepted, after some hesitation, the dignity of Cardinaldeacon of S. George in Velabro at the hands of Pope Leo XIII. He was allowed to reside at his Oratory in Birmingham and lived his remaining days in peace and sanctity, dying in 1890 at the age of eighty-nine.

Cardinal Newman's legacy of spiritual literature is probably the richest bequest of its kind England has ever received. To the general public the *Apologia* and *The Dream of Gerontius* are his best-known works. This is not the place to analyse Newman's work or the effect of his conversion and subsequent influence upon the Catholic Church in England, and so upon the future history of England. We are too close to see these things in proper perspective.

IV. EDWARD HENRY HOWARD

When Newman was created Cardinal 1879, the Sacred College contained the unusual number of three Englishmen. The second (Cardinal Manning being the first) was Edward Henry Howard, a great-grandson of the twelfth Duke of Norfolk and thus the second of his name and family to be a Cardinal. During all that period following the restoration of the hierarchy, which Newman called the ' Second Spring,' Howard was in the service of the papal court, remote from the controversies and developments in his native land. He thus completed the renewal of English participation in the government of the Church, representing a return to the tradition established by the Breakspears, Curzon, and Somercote in pre-Schism days, and followed in our own day by Cardinal Gasquet.

He was born at Nottingham early in the year of the Emancipation Act. Educated at Oscott and Edinburgh, he served as an officer in the 2nd Life Guards before turning to the priesthood. After studying at the Accademia Ecclesiastica with the future Cardinals Manning and Vaughan he was ordained by Cardinal Wiseman at the English College in 1854. Though his intentions were originally towards missionary work he was retained in Rome and attached to the household of Pope Pius IX. Here he became an expert linguist, mastering Arabic, Coptic and Hindustani. He was sent to India for a year on a mission to end the Goa Schism.

In 1872 he was consecrated titular Archbishop of Neocæsarea, and five years later Cardinal-priest of SS. John and Paul on the Cœlian Hill. Later he became Archpriest of the Basilica and Prefect of Congregation of S. Peter, and in 1884 Cardinal-Bishop of Frascati, thus ranking above both his great English contemporaries in the Sacred College.

Owing to ill-health he returned to England and died at Hatch Beauchamp, Brighton, in 1892. He was buried in the Fitzalan Chapel at Arundel beside his kinsman Blessed Philip Howard, martyr.

HERBERT CARDINAL VAUGHAN

V. HERBERT ALFRED VAUGHAN

When Cardinal Manning died, mourned by all England, he was succeeded in the Archbishopric of Westminster by Herbert Alfred Vaughan, a son of an old Catholic family which had suffered much for the Faith and the Stuart cause. He was born at Gloucester in 1832, about the time the Oxford Movement was commencing. Educated principally by the Jesuits at Stonyhurst and Brugelette, he spent one year at Downside and proceeded to Rome, where he met Manning and Howard. He was ordained at Lucca in 1854. In the following year he was Vice-president of S. Edmund's, Ware, and joined the Oblates of S. Charles, under Manning, two years later.

Vaughan's ill-health preventing him from undertaking missionary work as he desired, he decided to found a college for missionaries in England. To raise money for this purpose he went to America and the Caribbean Sea in 1863, and in the cause of his travels did heroic work during the smallpox epidemic in Panama, despite the opposition of the civil authorities. Having collected a substantial amount of money, he was recalled by Archbishop Manning, who had now succeeded Wiseman. He founded S. Joseph's Missionary College at Mill Hill and sent out the first missionaries to the American negroes. Having learned the value of the press in America, he bought and edited *The Tablet.*

As Bishop of Salford from 1872, he opened a seminary and founded S. Bede's College, Manchester. Throughout his life he was a zealous educationist, starting the Voluntary Schools Association in 1871, and was foremost in securing State aid for Catholic schools in the Education Act of 1902. He also founded the 'Rescue and Protection Society' for building homes and poor-law schools for Catholics.

When Cardinal Manning died in 1892 Bishop Vaughan succeeded him as Archbishop of Westminster and in the title of Cardinal-priest of SS. Andrew and Gregory on the Cœlian Hill. He had neither the personality nor the fighting spirit of his two predecessors, but he took full advantage of the opportunities for restoration and reconstruction in the period of comparative calm that followed the storms of their careers. He appointed the Commission on Anglican Orders which resulted in the declaration of their invalidity by the Bull of 1896.

His most outstanding work as Metropolitan was to begin the building of Westminster Cathedral in 1895. He died in 1903, having lived well to his motto, *Amare et Servare,* and was buried, by his own wish, in the grounds of his foundation at Mill Hill.

VI. AIDAN GASQUET

With Cardinal Gasquet we return to the old tradition of Catholic England, when English scholars ranked with the highest in the Church. He was born in London in 1846, the third son of Raymond Gasquet, Doctor of Medicine, and educated at the Benedictine School of S. Gregory attached to the Abbey of Downside. He entered the Benedictine Order at Belmont in 1865, was professed monk at Downside in 1871 and ordained priest three years later. He was Abbot of Downside from 1878 to 1885, and on relinquishing the office commenced the exhaustive historical researches for which he became world-famous.

From 1900–14 he was Abbot-President of the English Benedictines, and at the end of that term he was created by Pope Pius X Cardinal-deacon, with Cardinal Newman's title of S. George in Velabro, exchanging the title two years later for that of S. Maria in Campitelli. His very numerous works deal mainly with medieval English history and the period preceding the Reformation, the best known to the public being *Henry VIII and the English Monasteries*. His most important work was accomplished as Prefect of the Vatican Archives and President of the International Commission for the revision of the Vulgate, a work in

which he was still actively engaged up to the time
of his death in 1929. He was promoted to Cardinal-priest of S. Maria in Porticu in 1924.

VII. Francis Bourne

The present Cardinal-Archbishop of Westminster, the only Englishman now in the Sacred
College, was born at Clapham, London, in 1861,
the son of Henry Bourne, a civil servant and
a convert to the Faith, and Ellen, the daughter
of John Byrne, a Dublin merchant. He was
educated at S. Cuthbert's, Ushaw, S. Edmund's,
Ware, S. Sulpice, Paris, and the University of
Louvain. After his ordination in 1884 he was
curate successively at Blackheath, Mortlake and
West Grinstead in the diocese of Southwark, relinquishing parochial work to found, at the call
of Bishop Butt, the diocesan seminary of S. John
at Wonersh, of which he became first rector in
1889. He was made domestic prelate to Pope
Leo XIII in 1895, titular Bishop of Epiphania
and coadjutor to the Bishop of Southwark in 1896.
As Bishop of Southwark from 1897 to 1903 he
was responsible for the inauguration of the social
and rescue work which has since become famous.

He succeeded Cardinal Vaughan as Archbishop
of Westminster in 1903. He holds the honorary

FRANCIS CARDINAL BOURNE

degrees of Doctor of Theology and Philosophy at Louvain and D.C.L. Oxford. He was created Cardinal-priest in 1911 in the title of S. Pudentiana, formerly held by Cardinals Wiseman and Boso Breakspear.

PART III

IRISH, AMERICAN AND COLONIAL
CARDINALS

CHAPTER VII

THE ENGLISH-SPEAKING WORLD

I. PAUL CULLEN

THE first Irish Cardinal was not created until 1867, after the death of Cardinal Wiseman. We may safely ignore the very doubtful case of Archbishop John Comyn of Dublin, said (with no clear authority) to have been created in 1181. It is a strange fact that for so many centuries no representative of Catholic Ireland had a place in the Sacred College. Since personal qualifications were never lacking the omission must be attributed to the singularly subservient and nationally unimportant position to which Ireland was relegated under English domination.

Cardinal Wiseman was Irish by family, but he was born in Spain and must be regarded as English by education and adoption. Paul Cullen was Irish born and educated, and remained throughout his ministry a typical representative Irishman, despite his strong ultramontanism and his opposition to popular movements of revolt.

He was the son of a farmer in County Kildare. His early ability gained him admission to the College of Propaganda in 1820, being then seventeen. He had a brilliant career there as a classical and oriental scholar, eventually occupying the Chairs of Hebrew and Sacred Scripture and taking charge of the printing establishment of the Sacred Congregation. At twenty-five he received his doctorate at the hands of the Pope after a remarkable series of theses in defence of theology in a public disputation, though he was not ordained priest until the following year. Seven years later, in 1832, he was rector of the Irish College, and during his subsequent years in Rome he became an intimate friend of Pope Gregory XVI, and afterwards of Pope Pius IX. During the Roman revolution he was appointed rector of the College of Propaganda and saved it from Mazzini by placing it under the protection of the American minister, on the score of the American students. The year following he was consecrated Archbishop of Armagh and Primate of Ireland by the Cardinal-prefect of Propaganda. One of his first acts as Primate was to convene the important Synod of Thurles in 1850, the year of the restoration of the hierarchy in England. He presided at this synod in his capacity of apostolic delegate, being the first in Ireland for over two centuries.

After three years at Armagh, Archbishop Cullen

was transferred to the See of Dublin. For twenty-eight years he was foremost in the public life of his country, and he did great work for religious and secular education.

He vigorously opposed the attempts of the Protestant and Presbyterian factions to use the government land system against the Catholics. In politics he was constitutionalist, and by no means sympathetic with the more restive of the population. It is only fair to add that he did not suffer quite the same from English oppression. He interposed with the British Government to save General Thomas Burke from hanging. His chief concern was for the foundation of a Catholic University for Ireland, for which he had the powers of apostolic delegate, and he may justly be regarded as founder. Of this very difficult establishment, a constant focus of political contention, Dr. John Henry Newman was first rector, but the task was too much for such a man in the turbulent conditions prevailing.

So far as the Church in Ireland was concerned it enjoyed unparalleled prosperity under its first Cardinal. He was a strong disciplinarian whose discipline began with himself.

Archbishop Cullen was created Cardinal-priest of S. Pietro in Montorio in 1867. At the Vatican Council by desire of the Central Commission he proposed the definition of papal infallibility which

N

was finally accepted. A second great Irish Synod, that of Maynooth, was held under his presidency in 1875. He died in 1878 and was buried at his foundation of the Holy Cross at Clonliffe.

II. EDWARD McCABE

When in the last years of his long life Cardinal Cullen became too infirm to cope with the work of his office, he had the assistance of a coadjutor, Edward McCabe, titular Bishop of Gadara, consecrated in 1877. On the Cardinal's death he succeeded to the Archbishopric of Dublin and followed his predecessor's policy very closely. He was even more distrustful of popular movements, and he was so strongly constitutionalist, and active in supporting the administration from Dublin Castle, that he was long known as the ' Castle Bishop.' He had no sympathy with the Land League and naturally enough he was never popular with the Irish leaders. In furtherance of Cardinal Cullen's work he was responsible for a famous circular on University Education for Catholics. Notwithstanding his Castle sympathies he returned a vigorous answer to Judge Keogh's strong castigation of the clergy in the matter of the Galway election, when three bishops and thirty-one priests were reported guilty of intimidation and the elected

Home Ruler, Captain Nolan, was unseated in consequence.

Archbishop McCabe's constitutionalism was undoubtedly a conscientious matter of policy and it had the support of the Vatican. He was himself, like Cullen who preceded him and Cardinal Logue who followed him in the Sacred College, a man of the people. He was born in 1816 of poor parents in Dublin and educated at Father Doyle's school on the Quays, going thence to Maynooth. In 1839 he was curate at Clontarf, and later, as an assistant in the Cathedral parish, came under the notice of Archbishop Cullen. In 1854 he was offered and declined the Bishopric of Grahamstown, South Africa, preferring to remain in Dublin, where he obtained the parish of S. Nicholas Without. His parish work throughout his career was exceptionally industrious.

He was created Cardinal-priest in 1882, and died at the age of sixty-nine, three years later.

III. MICHAEL LOGUE

Michael Logue, Cardinal-priest of S. Maria della Pace, was the son of obscure parents in Raphoe. He became Bishop of his native diocese at the age of thirty-four, having occupied the Chairs of Theology and Belles-Lettres at the Irish College,

Paris. That alone marks him a man of unusual ability. Thereafter he was not primarily distinguished for his talents or his scholarship, but for more plebeian qualities. He became the most talked-of and most popular man in Ireland because he was so essentially and naturally Irish, typical of all that was traditionally ideal in the Irish priesthood. He was a lovable and human prelate with a great sense of humour, the subject of numberless stories. As a speaker and preacher he was direct, simple, and always witty.

At Raphoe he had the heavy and distressing task of alleviating the want and suffering during the Great Famine, and in one year alone he raised £30,000 for that purpose.

In 1887 he was made titular Bishop of Anazarbus and coadjutor to the Archbishop of Armagh, succeeding to the Primacy in the same year. He proceeded at once with the completion of the new Metropolitan Cathedral.

He was elevated to the Cardinalate in 1893, taking the title formerly held by Cardinal Acton. During his exceptionally long life and episcopal career, he was thirty-seven years Archbishop and thirty-one Cardinal, he exercised a wide influence on the affairs of his country. He died at Armagh in 1924, aged eighty-four, being the second senior member of the College of Cardinals.

IV. PATRICK O'DONNELL

Cardinal Logue's successor, Patrick O'Donnell, like his predecessors a man of the people, was born at Kilraine, County Donegal, on November 28, 1856, and educated at the Catholic University of Ireland and Maynooth. His ability gained him the Chair of Theology and the Prefecture at Dunboyne at the early age of twenty-three, and eventually he succeeded to the rectorship of the Catholic University. In 1888, being yet only thirty-two, he followed Archbishop Logue as Bishop of Raphoe, which See he held for the remarkable period of thirty-four years. In 1922 he became coadjutor to the Cardinal Primate and was consecrated titular Archbishop of Attalia. He succeeded to Armagh in 1924 and was elevated to the Sacred College in the following year in the title of S. Maria de Pace.

Cardinal O'Donnell was one of the most vigorous figures in ecclesiastical and political Ireland, but though a strong Nationalist (all his pastorals were published in both Irish and English) he was, like his predecessors, conservative and firmly constitutional. Throughout his life he worked for the cultivation of Irish unity, and it was he who presided at the great Convention of 1896 when the Nationalist forces were united under John

Redmond after the break-up following the Parnell affair. He was personally a man of tall, dignified presence and great charm, universally respected by non-Catholics as well as Catholics, and the trusted friend and adviser of the Irish Party.

As Primate, Cardinal O'Donnell summoned the important Plenary Synod of the Irish hierarchy at Maynooth in 1927, and it is probable that he was personally responsible for the canonical regulations then drawn up respecting the standard of living amongst the clergy. He died in his third year as Primate in 1927, being succeeded in the following year by Joseph MacRory, Bishop of Down and Connor.

V. JOSEPH MACRORY

The present Cardinal-Archbishop of Armagh, Joseph MacRory, was born at Ballygawley, County Tyrone, in 1861, educated at Armagh and Maynooth and ordained in 1885. In the following year he became Professor of Moral Theology and Sacred Scripture at Oscott, and in 1889 Professor of Sacred Scripture and Oriental Languages at Maynooth. In 1905 he was appointed to the Chair of Hermeneutics and New Testament Exegesis at the same seminary, where he became Vice-President in 1912.

In 1915 he was consecrated Bishop of Down

and Connor and translated to the Archbishopric
of Armagh to succeed Cardinal O'Donnell in 1928.
He was elevated to the Sacred College with the
title of S. John at the Latin Gate on December 16,
1929.

Cardinal MacRory has a wide reputation as a
scriptural scholar and is the author of many pub-
lications on the Gospel of S. John and other scriptural subjects. He holds the honorary degree of
D.Litt. at Queen's University, Belfast.

VI. JOHN McCLOSKY

The first American Cardinal was the son of Irish
parents, Patrick McClosky and Elizabeth, née
Hassen, who went to New York from Dungiven,
Co. Derry, in 1808, two years before John was
born at Brooklyn. Despite his persistently delicate health he had a brilliant early career and lived
to the ripe age of seventy-five.

He was educated at a small classical school kept
by Thomas Brady, and afterwards at Mount S.
Mary's College for the priesthood. In 1834 he
was the first New York born man to be ordained
secular priest. After a year as Professor of Philosophy at the new college at Nyack on the Hudson,
where he soon achieved distinction by his elo-
quence, he spent two years in Rome. There he

had the good fortune to be admitted to the friendship of a distinguished group, including Cardinal Weld, the future Cardinals Wiseman and Cullen, and the celebrated Père Lacordaire.

On returning to America he had considerable difficulties in his parish of S. Joseph's, Sixth Avenue, the trustees objecting to his youth and refusing to acknowledge him. He lived down their opposition and thenceforward his career was brilliantly successful. He was in due course first President of S. John's, Fordham, titular Bishop of Axière and coadjutor with right of succession to Bishop Hughes of New York (at thirty-four), and then Bishop of Albany, a new diocese of 30,000 square miles. The organization of this See in which he spent seventeen years may be regarded as his *chef d'œuvre*. He became the second Archbishop of New York in 1864 and Cardinal-priest of S. Maria supra Minervam in 1875.

VII. JAMES GIBBONS

The episcopal life of James Gibbons from 1868 to 1921 synchronized with an amazing expansion of the Church in the United States. An intense patriot, he was always to the fore in American public life, and his great popularity testifies to the value of his work to the nation.

Like so many other great prelates of his day in

America, he came of Irish parents. He was born
in Baltimore in 1834. After early education in
Ireland he returned to America to S. Charles College, Ellicott City. Thence he proceeded to a
business career, but fortunately changed his mind
at the age of twenty, after attending a Redemp-
torist Mission, and entered S. Mary's College,
Baltimore.

His priesthood began in war-time, 1861, and
being a Union man he served as chaplain. As
Bishop of Adramytum *in partibus* and Vicar-Apostolic of North Carolina he was the youngest bishop
at the Vatican Council 1869–70. In 1872 he was
Bishop of Richmond, and five years later he was
successively Bishop of Junopolis and Archbishop
of Baltimore. He presided as apostolic delegate
at the third Plenary Council of Baltimore and was
created Cardinal-priest of S. Maria in Trastevere
in 1886.

He did great work for education and as a medi-
ator in labour disputes. His three books, *Faith of
Our Fathers*, *Our Christian Heritage* and *The
Ambassador of Christ*, are still very widely read.

VIII. WILLIAM HENRY O'CONNELL

William Henry was the fourth son and eleventh
child of John O'Connell and Bridget, née Farley.
He was born at Lavell, Massachusetts, in 1859.

His early interests were in chemistry and medicine, but he eventually studied for the priesthood at Rome and was ordained in 1884. His first work was that of assistant priest at S. Joseph's, Medford, Mass., and as a young priest he did notable work in hospitals. In 1895 he became rector of the American College at Rome, and there first displayed his considerable financial acumen to effect in rescuing the college from bankruptcy and restoring it to prosperity. As Archbishop of Boston he was responsible for the extraordinary development of charitable institutions and a very considerable increase in Church property.

When he was consecrated Bishop of Portland, Maine, in 1901, he received an unprecedented official state welcome to Maine. Four years later he was sent as special papal envoy from Pope Pius X to the Emperor of Japan, his success on the occasion being crowned by the award of the Japanese Order of the Sacred Treasury.

He was made coadjutor to the Archbishop of Boston on the conclusion of his Japanese mission and succeeded Archbishop Williams in 1907. His first published work was his early lectures at the Catholic Summer School and he was later responsible for the publication of the translation of the *Life of Christ* by Cardinal de Lai.

He was created Cardinal-priest of S. Clemente at the same consistory as Cardinal Farley in 1911,

Under his rule the archdiocese of Boston has enjoyed remarkable prosperity and become famous for its contributions to the support of foreign missions and the propagation of the Faith.

A notable feature of his period of office has been the development of the Guild of S. Luke and similar philanthropic guilds.

IX.   JOHN FARLEY

A native of Newton Hamilton, County Armagh, John Farley passed his youth in Ireland before emigrating to New York. After a period at S. John's College, Fordham, and the seminary at Troy, where he became an expert mathematician and linguist, he went to the American College, Rome, for three years. A distinctive note of his scholastic career was his keen interest in English literature, and he achieved considerable facility in writing verse.

After his ordination in 1870 he did two years' parochial work at New Brighton before becoming secretary to Archbishop McClosky of New York, whose life he wrote later. In 1884 he became domestic prelate with charge of the parish of S. Gabriel, East 37th Street, where he did great work for the development of Catholic schools, and instituted parochial visitation of all parishioners by the clergy. As Vicar-General and later as titular Bishop of Zeugma and auxiliary he worked hard for the seminaries and education generally. He succeeded to the Archbishopric of New York in 1903, and followed his early patron, Cardinal McClosky, in the title of Cardinal-priest of S. Maria supra Minervam in 1911.

As Archbishop he obtained a greater share of monsignorial honours for his clergy, and in doing so is said to have made half his diocese purple and the other half blue—though his greatest desire was no doubt to see it inviolate.

By his organization of a mass protest meeting he had much effect in reducing the religious persecution in France. He was a prime mover in the foundation of the *Catholic Encyclopædia*. He died in 1918.

X. DENIS DOUGHERTY

Born of Irish parents at Guardville, Schyllkill County, Pennsylvania, in 1865, Cardinal Dougherty was educated at the public schools of Ashland and Girardville before proceeding to S. Mary's College (of the Society of Jesus) at Montreal and thence to S. Charles' Seminary, Overbrook, Pa. He completed his sacerdotal training at the North American College, Rome, and was ordained in 1890, receiving his Doctorate of Divinity at Propaganda, and proceeding to a Chair at S. Charles' Seminary forthwith.

DENIS CARDINAL DOUGHERTY

In 1903 he was consecrated Bishop of Nueva Segovia in the Philippine Islands, being the first American to hold the office. Here he achieved notable missionary success and effective organization of the Church, dealing very successfully with the havoc wrought by the Aglipayan schism. He was translated to the See of Jaro, in the province of Iloilo, P.I., in 1908, and seven years later to the See of Buffalo, where he showed great administrative ability. In 1918 he succeeded to the Archbishopric of Philadelphia, one of the most important of the American dioceses in size and organization, and important educational advances have been an outstanding feature of his administration.

Archbishop Dougherty was created Cardinal-priest of SS. Nereus and Achilleis on the Appian Way in 1921, and he is known to have great devotion to S. Thérèse of Lisieux.

XI. PATRICK HAYES

The present Cardinal-Archbishop of New York was born in the Lower East side of New York City, within half a mile of Governor Al. Smith and Cardinal Mundelein, in 1867. He was educated at the schools of the Christian Brothers, the De La Salle Institute, Manhattan College, Troy, and the Catholic University of America. Ordained

in 1892 he commenced his priesthood as curate at
S. Gabriel's under the future Cardinal Farley, to
whom as Bishop Farley he was afterwards secretary. In 1903 he was first President of the Cathedral College and Chancellor of the Archdiocese,
becoming domestic prelate four years later, and
titular Bishop of Tagasta, auxiliary to the Archbishop, in 1914. In 1917 he was appointed Ordin-
ary of all Catholics in the United States Army and
Navy, with a seat on the National War Council,
and in 1920 he was Chaplain-in-Chief, receiving
the dignity of Chevalier du Legion d'Honneur
and the Order of the Crown of Italy.

He succeeded to the Archbishopric in 1919 and
was created Cardinal-priest of S. Maria in Via in
1924 at the same consistory as Cardinal Mundelein.
He has been prominently associated with every
sort of patriotic undertaking, and his administration has been notable for the great reorganization
of charitable works in New York.

XII. George Mundelein

The only American Cardinal who was not of
Irish extraction, the Cardinal of Chicago, was born
in New York. His family, though German in
origin, was profoundly American, his grandfather
having been killed serving in the Union ranks at

PATRICK CARDINAL HAYES

Fort Sumter. He was five years younger than
Patrick Hayes, and followed him through the De
La Salle Institute and Manhattan College, From
there he went to S. Vincent's Benedictine College
at Beatty, Pa., and then to the College of Propaganda, being ordained in Rome in 1895. His first
charge was the Lithuanian Church in the Eastern
district of Brooklyn. He became Chancellor of
the Brooklyn diocese in 1897, censor of the Litur-
gical Academy in 1903 and domestic prelate in
1906.

As a result of his brilliant defence of Pope Pius
X's *Condemnation of Modernism* he was the first
American to be made a member of the Ancient
Academy of Arcadia, and at the Pope's jubilee he
was made Doctor of Sacred Theology by the
Congregation of Propaganda. He was titular
Bishop of Laryma and auxiliary of Brooklyn in
1909, and Archbishop of Chicago in 1915, at the
age of forty-three ; with Archbishop Hayes, he
was created Cardinal-priest in 1924 with the title
of S. Maria del Popolo.

Cardinal Mundelein is well known as an organ-
izer and director of the social life of his metropolis.
He built the already famous seminary of S. Mary
of the Lake, the scene of the great Eucharistic
Congress of 1925, and he made a notable depar-
ture from precedent in staffing it with professors
of the Society of Jesus.

XIII.   JEAN-LOUIS DE CHEVERUS

Cardinal de Cheverus was the first Bishop of
Boston. He was called to Boston by a former
tutor in 1796 when he was teaching for a living
in London after his escape from Paris in disguise
during the Revolution. In New England he
worked unceasingly among the sick and poor and
lived among the Red Indians and learned their
language. His devotion and humility won the
respect of the Puritans so completely that they
invited him to preach in their pulpits. The legis-
lature recognized his brilliance and his wisdom to
the extent of regarding him as an adviser.

With funds he collected he built a church in
Boston, and in 1808 he was named Bishop, being
consecrated two years later. Eventually on account
of ill-health he was recalled to his native France,
despite the protests of all Boston, and translated
to the See of Montauban. Before long this Huguenot stronghold felt the influence of his great holiness and charity, and a prominent citizen declared
that the Montaubans were ' now all the Bishop's
men.' He was raised to the Archbishopric of
Bordeaux and created a peer by Charles X. In
1836, the year of his death, Pope Gregory XVI
made him Cardinal-priest.

XIV. PATRICK MORAN

Patrick Francis Moran, third Archbishop of Sydney and first Cardinal of Australia, is one of the most outstanding figures in the history of the Commonwealth. It is hardly an exaggeration to say that he contributed more than any other man to the foundation of modern Australia. He forecasted and urged the necessity for the Australian Federation, the navy and the citizen soldiery. The many monuments to his memory testify to the esteem in which he was held by all parties.

He was born in Ireland, at Leighlinbridge, in 1830, the only son of Patrick Moran and Alice Cullen, sister of the Cardinal. Orphaned at an early age he was sent to study in Rome. He became vice-rector of the Irish College, Professor of Hebrew at Propaganda and vice-rector of the Scots College. From being secretary to his uncle the Cardinal, whom he accompanied to the Vatican Council and to whose influence he owed a great deal, he became Bishop of Olba *in partibus* and coadjutor to the Bishop of Ossory.

As an Irishman he was a vigorous champion of Home Rule and proved himself a capable diplomat.

He was translated to Sydney as Archbishop, being Pope Leo XIII's personal choice, in 1884, and created Cardinal-priest of S. Susanna in the following year. His pastoral work was amazing

o

in extent—he founded no less than thirty-two charities besides new parishes and schools in Sydney. He died at Manly in 1911.

XV. ELZEAR-ALEXANDRE TASCHEREAU

Canada's first Cardinal was true Canadian born and bred of an old French settler family, and he lived and died in his native Quebec. He graduated after a brilliant course at the Seminary of Quebec and proceeded to Rome, where he had serious intentions of becoming a Benedictine, but did not do so. He was ordained priest at his home town, La Beauce, and remained at the seminary as Professor. A keen educationist, he was one of the founders of Laval University. He visited Rome again in 1854 to take the degree of Doctor of Canon Law at the French Seminary, and yet again in 1869 as theologian to Archbishop Baillargeon at the Vatican Council.

On his return to Canada in 1871 he was made Archbishop of Quebec, and he proved himself a great administrator, founding many new parishes and missions. Of a silent disposition he was yet a voluminous writer, his published discourses, pastorals, and other letters occupying six volumes of 900 pages each. He also wrote the history of the Seminary of Quebec.

He was created Cardinal-priest of S. Maria della Vittoria in 1886 and died in 1898, greatly venerated by his clergy and his people. The full extent of his work in Quebec can hardly yet be gauged, but there is no doubt that his quiet profound influence had an effect on the Dominion far beyond the confines of Quebec.

XVI. Louis-Nazaire Bégin

Louis-Nazaire Bégin, like his predecessor Cardinal Taschereau, was born and bred in his diocese of Quebec.

After passing through the local school of his birthplace, Levis, and the Commercial College of S. Michael, he entered the Quebec Seminary, taking the degree of B.A. and becoming Prince of Wales Prizeman of Laval University. After his ordination in Rome and taking his Doctorate of Theology at Innsbruck he held several academic posts at Quebec at the Seminary, Laval University and the École Normale. He was consecrated Bishop of Chicoutimi in 1888, and three years later titular Archbishop of Cyrene and coadjutor to the Cardinal-Archbishop of Quebec, whom he succeeded in 1898. He was made Cardinal-priest of SS. Vitalis, Gervase and Protase in 1914 and died in 1925.

Cardinal Bégin, during his early episcopate,

played a vigorous part in the struggle of the Canadian bishops in defence of Catholic schools of Manitoba against the oppressive enactment of 1890. As Archbishop he created many new parishes and welcomed numerous religious orders, both of men and women, to his diocese. He wrote several able works, notably on Infallibility, the rule of Faith, and veneration of the Saints.

XVII. RAYMOND MARIE ROULEAU

A native of Quebec like his two predecessors, Cardinals Taschereau and Bégin, Raymond Marie Rouleau, Archbishop of Quebec, was born at Isle Verte in 1866. He was one of eleven children of Felix Rouleau and Luce Irvine. Educated at the Seminary of Rimouski he entered the Order of Preachers at the age of twenty and was ordained at Corte, Corsica, six years later. He was first prior of the Dominicans at Ottawa in 1900 and became Provincial of the Canadian Province in 1919. In 1923 he was consecrated Bishop of Valleyfield, Que., and apostolic delegate in the same year, being translated to Quebec as Archbishop in 1926. He received the pallium and entered the Sacred College as Cardinal-priest of S. Pietro in Montorio in the following year. In 1929 he was elected Knight Grand Cross of the Order of the Holy Sepulchre. He died in May, 1931.

INDEX

Abelard, 4
Acherus, 34
Acton, Charles, 150–152
Adrian IV, 5–11
Adrian VI, 97
Agnes, S., 14
Albertus Magnus, 42 et seq.
Alcuin of York, 3
Alexander III, 11, 13, 15
Allen, William, 135–138
American College (Rome), 190–191
Anglo-Catholics, 162 et seq.
Anglus, Thomas, 35
Anti-Popes :
  Clement VII, 53, 133
  Benedict XIII, 63
Aquinas, S. Thomas, 37, 39, 42 et seq.
Aragon, Catherine of, 99, 110–113, 121
Armada, The, 138
Aristotle, 37
Arnold of Brescia, 9
Arras, Conference at, 73, 76
Aske, Robert, 119
Augustine, S., 18, 37
Australian Commonwealth, 197

Bainbridge, Christopher, 88–90
Beaton, David, 131–135
Beaufort, Henry, 6, 60, 64–74 et seq.
Becket, S. Thomas à, 11–15
Bégin, Louis-Nazaire, 199–200
Belloc, H., 9
Benedict XI, 39
Berardus, 34
Bishops, in fifteenth and sixteenth centuries, 78–79
Blackfriars, Synod of, 57
Boleyn, Anne, 99, 131
Boniface VIII, 43
Boniface IX, 53
Bornhem Priory, 140
Bosham, Herbert of, 13–15
Botoner, William, 82
Bourchier, Thomas, 77–82
Bourne, Francis, 174–175
Bray, William, 34
Breakspear, Boso, 11–14
Breakspear, Nicholas, 5–11, 15 et seq., 107
Bristow, Dr., 138
Browning, Robert, 158

201

Logue, Michael, 183–184
Lollards, 57, 59, 109
Louis XII, 95
Lucius II, 4
Lucius III, 15
Luther, Martin, 98, 109

Macclesfield, William, 39
MacRory, Joseph, 186–187
McCabe, Edward, 182–183
McClosky, John, 187–188, 191
Magna Carta, 23 *et seq.*
Manning, Henry, 159–165
Marcellus II, 125
Margaret, Countess of Salisbury, 120
Mary I (of England), 122–127
Mary Queen of Scots, 133 *et seq.*
Martin V, 67–70
Matthew of Westminster, 32
Milner, Bishop, 149, 155
Moran, Patrick, 197–198
More, Bl. Thomas, 83, 84, 88, 108, 117, 129
Morton, John, 83–88
Mundelein, George, 194–195

Napoleon, 147
Newman, John Henry, 154, 160, 165–169
Tract XC, 160–161, 166
Nicholas I, Czar, 152
Nicholas V, 77

Oates, Titus, 142

Oblates of S. Charles, 163, 171
O'Connell, William, 189–191
O'Donnell, Patrick, 185–186
Orders, Religious :
Augustinians, 57
Benedictines, 47, 51, 84, 173
Brigittines, 129
Carthusians, 129
Dominicans, 36, 37, 43, 138, 140, 200
Franciscans, 43, 129
Oscott Seminary, 155, 157, 170, 186
Osney, Synod at, 28
Oxford Movement, the, 155 *et seq.*

Palmerston, Lord, 158
Pandulph, 21–24 *et seq.*
Papacy, the, 5–14, 63, 88
Liber Pontificalis, 14
Gesta Romanorum Pontificum, 14
at Avignon, 45, 46
Papal infallibility, 164, 168, 181
Paris, Matthew, 31
Paris, University of, 29, 30
Parnell, 185
Parsons, Robert, 135
Paul II, 81
Paul III, 114, 116, 121
Paul IV, 125, 130
Peckham, Archbishop, 38
Peter the Hermit, 21 *et seq.*

The Mayflower Press, Plymouth.   William Brendon & Son, Ltd.